THE LAYMANS GUIDE
AVOIDANCE OF CARE CHARGES

SELF DEFENCE FOR ASSETS

USING PRACTICAL AND

LEGAL TECHINQUES

NORTH TYNESIDE LIBRARIES	
BARCODE 01530 1469	
CLASS 362.61	
LIB How	LOC
INV DATE 9.12.06	CHECKED

CONTENTS

Contents	page 5
Introduction	page 11
General Explanations – Part 1	page 15
Making a Refund Claim	page 33
General – Part 2	page 36
Introduction to the Problem	page 37
Protection of Capital Assets	page 39

PROTECTION OF CAPITAL

Options -		page 41
1].	Abuse of Power	page 41
2].	Affordability	page 44
3].	Annuity	page 45
4].	Business Interests	page 46
5].	Care Fee Insurance	page 47
6].	Carer in occupation of property	page 48
7].	Conflict of Interest	page 48
8].	Constructive/Resulting Trusts	page 49
9].	Council House purchase	page 50
10].	Courts	page 52
11].	Declaration of Trust	page 52
12].	Disclaimer	page 53
13].	Divorce	page 56
14].	Equity Release	page 57
15].	Freehold/Leasehold property	page 59
16].	Funeral plans	page 60
17].	Healthcare Commission	page 61

18].	Home Care	page	62
19].	Human Rights Act 1998:-	page	63
	(A) Article 1	page	63
	(B) Article 3	page	64
	(C) Article 5	page	65
	(D) Article 7	page	66
	(E) Article 8	page	67
	(F) Article 14	page	69
20].	Investment	page	69
21].	Joint Bank Account	page	71
22].	Joint Freehold/Leasehold Property	page	72
23].	Licence	page	72
24].	Life Policies	page	73
25].	Lifetime Gifts (a)	page	74
26].	Lifetime Gifts (b)	page	76
27].	Limitation Act 1980	page	78
28].	Litigation	page	79
29].	MP (Member of Parliament)	page	82
30].	Marriage	page	83
31].	Medical Negligence	page	86
32].	Mental Health Act	page	86
33].	Move House	page	86
34].	NHS Funding Claim	page	88
35].	National Health Service & Community Care Act 1990	page	90
36].	Negligence (General)	page	92
37].	One spouse surviving at home	page	95
38].	Palfrey Case	page	96
39].	Pension Funds	page	97
40].	Personal Injury	page	99
41].	Pointon Case	page	99

42}.	Promissory Estopple	page 100
43].	Property in sole name of one spouse	page 103
44].	Proprietary Estopple	page 106
45].	Public Guardianship Office	page 113
46].	Public Interest/Public Policy	page 115
47].	Refusal	page 116
48].	Scottish System	page 118
49].	Severance of Joint Tenancy	page 118
50].	Social Care	page 120
51].	Spend Money	page 121
52].	Theft	page 123
53].	Trusts – General	page 125
54].	Trusts of Land and Appointment of Trustees Act 1996	page 126
55].	Variation	page 127
56].	Wills – Generally	page 129
57].	Wills – Mutual	page 131

PROTECTION OF INCOME   page 134

PROTECTION OF FUTURE ASSETS   page 141

Proprietary Estoppel –
 Inheritance Tax Planning   page 143
Proprietary Estoppel –
 Capital Gains Tax Planning   page 147

Miscellaneous Matters :-   page 148
A]. Avoidance   page 148
B]. Complaints   page 148
C]. Confidentiality   page 149
D]. Councils   page 149
E]. CRAG   page 150
F]. Enduring Powers of Attorney   page 151
G]. Foul Play   page 152
H]. Freedom of Information Act 2000   page 152
I]. Income Support/Pension Credit   page 153
J]. Legal Advice   page 154
K]. Mental Capacity law   page 155
L]. More trouble than its worth   page 155
M]. Probate Procedures   page 156
N]. Publicity   page 157
O]. Re-Assessments   page 158
P]. Refund Claim Timing   page 158
Q]. Sheltered Accommodation   page 158
R]. Strength in Numbers   page 159
S]. Wills – Professional Executors   page 160

Care Refund Claim Form   page 162

List of Statutes   page 166

Index   page 199

Index to Precedents		page 169
1).	Severance of Joint Tenancy	page 171
2).	Will Clause in confirmation of Declaration of Trust	page 173
3).	Will Clause in confirmation of Proprietary Estoppel	page 175
4).	Disclaimer	page 176
5).	Deed of Variation	page 179
6).	Will Clause giving effect to a Life interest	page 191
7).	Declaration of Trust	page 192
8).	Enduring Power of Attorney	page 197

INTRODUCTION

This book lists more than 50 legal, ethical and practical arguments and strategies that can be used to challenge a claim by a local council that they are entitled to take an individual's assets (both capital and or income) to fund care home fees. The issues covered in this book also include explanations of how to plan ahead by arranging financial and legal affairs in a way that protects assets and avoids them being used (or sold) to fund a care home or residential home placement.

Further details are also included in these pages relating to financial entitlements that should be provided under the National Health Service (via local Primary Care Trusts) to fund care costs in full or in part.

Precedents of standard relevant legal documentation are also included at the end of the book.

This book is not intended as a guide to those who wish to know the current system for the charging of individuals for their care. It is however intended as a source of information and guidance for those who wish to challenge the system of charging individuals for care by refusing to accept, comply or co-operate with the financial assessment procedure instigated by the local council.

The relevant "authorities" who may be challenged

include the Local Council, Central Government, Local Primary Care Trusts (PCT's), Strategic Area Health Authorities or anyone else who claims that it is right and proper in all the circumstances for them to obtain money or other assets belonging to a person who is in need of some form of professional care either at home, a nursing home or elsewhere.

This book is also intended as an aid to advice workers and professional practitioners such as lawyers, accountants and financial advisers who are asked to advise clients on what actions can be taken to protect assets from being used to fund care charges.

Many of the options described below overlap. This combined with the nature of the subject matter means that in order to fully understand and appreciate just what is possible and also determine which options are relevant to particular individuals it is recommended that all the options listed below are considered before reaching a final conclusion and embarking on a plan of action or defence.

Furthermore, as changes occur (particularly those relating to the health of the person in care) the list of useable options will similarly change perhaps over a brief period of time. Any change in circumstances of an intended eventual beneficiary of an asset should also be viewed as a time to reconsider all long term asset protection plans. Perhaps the obvious change for an intended beneficiary would be the consequences of a divorce, separation, bankruptcy or marriage.

The contents section above (pages 5 – 8) summarises the options available, although additional possibilities may arise and be relevant in particular local authority areas. To assist in identifying the most suitable options a photocopy of the four contents pages could be made and those which are unsuitable or irrelevant be deleted. The remaining options are the arguments/asset protection strategies to be used or upon which more detailed legal advice can be sought.

It should also be remembered that as each individual case will be different what may be a perfectly reasonable option for one person may be totally unsuitable for another.

The content of this book relates to the law in England and Wales and legal practice as at July 2006.

Where time permits, readers (and especially professional advisers) will also find it helpful to read the detailed case report of the judgement in the 1999 Coughlan case. Very brief details of this important case are mentioned below as the full text of the case would provide more than sufficient material to prepare a separate book.

Before the options below are considered in detail it is strongly recommended that readers first study the general explanations that are described in the Question and Answers section as this will assist in understanding the technical and legal principles that follow.

General Explanations – Part 1

Questions and Answers:-

Q : - What are Care Charges?

A : - Fees that are payable to an establishment which provides accommodation and other services to an individual, the establishment being the permanent or temporary residential address of the individual. (The word temporary will apply for example to those who are in respite care whilst their carer has a break).

Q : - Why do such care charges arise?

A : - As a result of increasing life expectancy more and more people find themselves in the unfortunate position that due to reasons of poor or failing mental and or physical health they are no longer able to remain independent by living at home, perhaps even with the assistance of a partner or spouse.

The individual's home may be a rented property (council, private or housing association), or an owner occupied private dwelling. The individual may live with another family member. The rented home may be some form of sheltered accommodation where the building is owned by the council or a private housing association or perhaps a charitable organisation. The individual may also be a patient who has been detained in a hospital under the provisions and authority of the Mental Health Act 1983.

Q : - Why is the subject of "care fees" such a contentious issue?

A : - There are two contrasting viewpoints:-

(A) On the one hand it can be argued that if an individual is unable to care for himself to the extent that professional assistance is required to provide some degree of care or supervision then it is not unreasonable as in the case of any other professional service that it should be paid for by the individual using that service.

(B) On the other hand the service that is being provided for payment is "care" which is invariably necessary on grounds of health. If the individual did not require such "care" then he or she would still be living at home. This care, at whatever level is necessary because the individual suffers from such a poor state of health (whether physical, mental or both) that they are prevented from taking care of their own needs and that carers who visit on a periodic basis are considered inadequate to provide the level of "care" required. The argument follows that those individuals admitted to 24 hour "care" who have provided a lifetime of work with the associated payment of countless direct and indirect taxes and national insurance contributions would not unreasonably expect to be provided with any required level of care without further financial cost or means testing. The logic and expectation is that such care costs have in reality already been paid for in advance by those very taxes and insurance.

The unfairness of the system is further evidenced by the fact that those who have little by way of assets receive all care of whatever nature as and when required without similar financial penalty.

Q : - When do such "charges" become relevant?

A : - It should be remembered that there are several types of "professional" care home. Broadly speaking they fit into one of five categories:-

    (i)   Residential Care Homes where no health care is provided.

(ii) Nursing Care homes where some degree of Health Care is provided from health care which is merely incidental to other so called "social" and personal care needs to highly specialist care from a nurse or other medically trained personnel.

Some care homes may be classed as E.M.I homes. These homes provide care to the Elderly Mentally Infirm.

(iii) NHS establishments such as hospitals. Some private care homes also provide NHS continuing care beds. The hospital may be a general hospital involving some form of health assessment or a specialist mental hospital where the individual is resident and possibly being detained with or without their consent.

(iv) A duel registered care home. Such homes provide both residential places and nursing care places in the same building but usually on different floors. Such homes may have general care beds and E.M.I. care beds.

(v) Hospices. There are no charges to the individual for such places as they rely on charitable donations.

The type of care which is assessed as being required is the most important aspect to the whole care fee charging regime. There are several basic types of individual situation:-

(i) Those individuals who are assessed as requiring only residential care. Such people will almost certainly be faced with the council Social Services department seeking to conduct a financial assessment as to all capital assets owned by the individual and his income.

(ii) Those individuals who are assessed as needing 24 hour care in a nursing home. Such people may not necessarily be granted NHS funding. Again such persons will be faced with the council Social Services department seeking to conduct a financial assessment as to the extent and precise nature of all their capital and income.

(iii) Those in NHS establishments should have no problem in terms of funding for their care as these places are free as they are part of the National Health Service. It is likely that prolonged periods in care will however result in a significant reduction or loss of other state benefits such as

Attendance Allowance and Disability Living Allowance until discharge.

(iv) Those who are placed in a duel registered home may be charged for care initially if they are placed in the residential section but then qualify for some form of funding on being moved to the nursing section if their health deteriorates with the corresponding result that the level of "nursing" care component increases.

(v) Those in a hospice are usually terminally ill and so should in theory be entitled to category one full funding from the local Primary Care Trust. The Hospice however is unlikely to make reference to the subject of funding.

(vi) Those who regardless of their state of health refuse admittance to a care home and prefer to remain at home.

Q : - What is meant by the phrase "some form of funding" in terms of those assessed as requiring 24 hour care?

A : - In order to address the whole subject of charging for care and in an attempt by government to mitigate the financial effects upon the individual a banding system was introduced.

At present there are several levels of health care component in the determination of any funding contribution by the NHS:-

There are:-

(a) Those who are assessed as having no health care needs. Result - no financial contribution from the local Primary Care Trust (i.e. the NHS). In practice this means that the Council seek wherever possible to obtain the assets (capital and income) of the individual.

(b) Those who are assessed as having nursing care needs. In this case the nursing care element of the care will be paid by the NHS. This amount is paid direct to the care home by the NHS. A registered nurse will usually conduct the assessment to determine which of the three banding levels apply.

The three banding levels (for the year 2006/07) are:-

(a) The low band which amounts to £40.00 per week. This is paid for those who require minimal registered nursing input.

(b) The medium band which amounts to £83.00 per week. This is paid for those who have multiple needs requiring care from a registered nurse on a daily basis and where the general state of health (mental and or physical) is stable and predictable.

(c) The high band of £133.00 per week. This is paid for those who have "complex" nursing care needs. This is defined as "mechanical, technical and/or therapeutic interventions throughout 24 hours and the overall state of mental and or physical health is unstable and or unpredictable".

In practice any such award may have no effect on the level of funding required from the individual as it has become common practice for some care homes to increase their fees by a corresponding amount when such a banding level is awarded. This of course cancels out the effect and benefit of the NHS banding payment to the effect that the individual is still required to make payment at the same level.

(e) The final category are those who receive the full amount of their care fees in the form of a payment direct from the Primary

Care Trust to the care home. It should be remembered that if someone qualifies for full funding this may not be permanent as any improvement in health will be identified during re-reassessment. This may result in the loss of all or part of the Primary Care Trust contribution. Therefore even when NHS funding is being paid steps should still be taken to safeguard as far as possible the other assets held by the individual in care, should the care funding be reduced or withdrawn.

It is a curious situation if not a contradiction that an individual can be assessed as qualifying for high band care funding because of complex and unpredictable care needs but the level of health is still considered sufficiently good so as to disqualify him from full care funding.

In any assessment as to a banding level it should not be assumed that the "eligibility criteria" used by the assessor to reach a decision is correct. In other words the person being assessed may be having a good day or may be under sedation more than usual or the criteria used may not be in accordance with official guidance from the Health Service Ombudsman, The Healthcare Commission or the Department of Health or for that matter the criteria may not even be correct in terms of the law itself.

Q :-   What is wrongful charging?

A :-   Those who are in care homes, and especially those receiving 24 hour care are the most likely to have been assessed incorrectly or not at all by the Social Services department of the local council. The person who conducted the assessment may not be known to the patient or his family or may not have spoken to anyone else involved in the matter such as a carer spouse or partner.

Those who have been in care for a period of several years are particularly at risk of being the victims of wrongful charging. This is because if the care placement was arranged before the introduction of the banding system and or before the publication of the Health Service Ombudsman's rulings in 2003 then only a proper re-assessment against correct eligibility criteria would discover the truth. It follows that those who have no family are particularly vulnerable to never learning the truth of being wrongfully charged.

The most recent regime which required those in care to provide the funding for their care arose from the National Health Service and Community Care Act 1990. The financial responsibility for the payment of care costs fundamentally changed with this Act. The responsibility shifted in April 1993 from social security (national taxation) to local councils (local taxation). This additional financial burden placed on local councils explains why council tax levels have increased so dramatically over the last few years as councils suddenly had to find huge additional funds to pay the care costs of those in residential and nursing care homes. There was no corresponding increase from central government to councils to cover the extra costs which then fell upon council tax payers. Another reason for the escalation of council tax levels is the introduction of the minimum wage which resulted in increases in the weekly care fees by 10% year on year.

This situation continued until the Coughlan case in 1999. The full name of the case is Coughlan v North and East Devon Health Authority. The critical issue that was considered by the Court was whether nursing care for a chronically ill patient may lawfully be provided by a local council as a social service (in which case the council would seek payment under means testing) or whether such care is required to be provided by law free of charge as part of the National Health Service. The Coughlan case dealt with a considerable number of issues on appeal by the Health Authority which had sought to challenge their previous failure in

Court that they could effectively pass the financial responsibility to the local council.

This case can however be cited as authority that a Primary Care Trust cannot pass its responsibility for the care of those who require nursing care to the council. The NHS is still liable in law to fund any care costs regardless of where that care is provided and the financial means of the individual requiring such care.

As a result of the above, local authorities (the then Local Health Authorities and District Councils) should have reviewed their assessment procedures. In reality little changed with the result that many people continued to be charged for their health care using the old outdated systems that had been in place for many years. Systems of assessment and eligibility still differ from area to area today. Councils have different assessment procedures and Primary Care Trusts operate to different eligibility criteria. The often used phrase post code lottery is therefore a reality for many as their place of residence rather than their state of health can determine whether they are charged for their care.

The situation improved dramatically in early 2003 with the publication of several Health Service Ombudsman's reports. The Ombudsman had decided several cases following detailed investigations which had been referred for complaint. The complaints had been lodged because the individuals being assessed had failed the local authority means test. The substance of the complaints were that individuals had been wrongfully charged for their care in that the individuals who had been assessed as being liable to pay for their own care had such a poor level of health that any and all care costs should be provided free of charge by the National Health Service. The Ombudsman agreed.

Of the four cases considered one case involved a man who suffered from Alzheimer's disease, two cases were of women who were severely disabled by strokes and one was a woman who suffered from Vascular Dementia.

This provided the first real opportunity to go back and challenge both Primary Care Trusts and local councils about their financial assessment procedures.

In these cases as the Ombudsman stated that the care charges related to health care then this was the responsibility of the NHS. As a result those who had paid fees were entitled to a refund from the Primary Care Trust.

Q :-   What is the present position?

A :-   One estimate on the internet suggests that the sum of £10 billion pounds has been wrongfully charged to those in care.

Despite the Ombudsman's rulings Social Service departments have still been slow to change their outdated and incorrect assessment procedures. The level of service provided by councils varies considerably around the Country as some councils apply their discretionary powers very harshly whilst others provide considerable assistance to individuals and their family to identify how assets can be preserved and what other sources of funding are available.

In the first instance when it is believed that someone has been wrongfully charged for their care contact should be made with the Primary Care Trust in which the claimant resided. In many cases the wrongfully charged person will have died and so it will fall upon their personal representative (Executor or Administrator) to make the claim. A person who is appointed as Enduring Power of Attorney or Receiver may also apply on behalf of a living person as their official legal representative.

Any person who holds the position of appointee for state benefit purposes should also apply as it is highly likely that pension income at the very least will have been used to contribute towards the care fees. The next of kin may also apply.

A word of caution however is that it is not unknown for Primary Care Trusts to request a next of kin to apply to be appointed receiver before the claim will be investigated. The only logical reason for this is to deter claims as it is unlikely that an individual will go to the trouble delay and expense of incurring more than a thousand pounds in costs without knowing whether a refund will be made. In this situation a complaint to the Health Services Ombudsman (or the Healthcare Commission for persons admitted to care since April 2004) is the best course of action.

Those who have been wrongfully charged care fees (or their representative) must take the initiative and make an application for a refund in the form of a complaint to the Primary Care Trust for the area in which the person in care lived. The whole process of making a refund claim is likely to result in a delay of many months if not more than a year whilst the Primary Care Trust investigates the complaint. It is therefore vital to be patient as the delay in itself can be a means of putting people off from progressing with the claim via the Area Strategic Health Authority and then the Ombudsman or

Healthcare Commission.

Q :- Is Timescale relevant?

A. Yes - Presently claims can go back to 1996. As a result for someone in care for several years the amount of refund could be considerable and therefore total several tens of thousands of pounds. In addition to the amount wrongfully charged a sum in respect of lost interest is also paid. Amounts paid for any period in care before 1996 are so far irrecoverable. There is however no reason why claims for periods prior to this cannot be made using one of more of the legal arguments detailed below.

Q :- What other sums can be claimed?

A :- The addition of interest to the claim refund amount is to compensate the person in care for the loss of the interest or income that would have been generated had the money not been taken to pay care fees. The amount of interest paid is however noticeably far lower that would be achievable as an average market rate. Furthermore, when a property has been sold it is unlikely that a claim would be entertained for the loss of capital that would have been held had the property not been sold. There is of course no harm in seeking such additional payment. Rather than the Primary Care Trust itself such a claim is probably better directed to the Council whose Social Services department conducted the means testing and even more so if the Council had been challenged at the time of their original financial assessment. In this situation it is difficult to argue that the Primary Care Trust is liable as they would have no knowledge of the assessed person's assets. The lodgement of a claim for negligence against the council would therefore be a starting point. If no satisfaction is obtained from the council then a complaint to the council under its complaints procedure for their failure to deal with the claim would be the next step. Following this a referral of the complaint to the Local Authority Ombudsman would be in order. A further complaint to your M.P. may also provoke some action. Membership of a consumer organisation may also be helpful.

Q : - If the law says that an individual must pay for his/her care if assessed to do so whether in full or in part how can this be challenged?

A :- In brief terms the law says many things some of which are contradictory. The rules relating to the assessed contribution or fully self funded care are open to considerable interpretation bearing in mind the large body of other laws and decided cases that have been considered by the courts over hundreds of years. A list of some of the other applicable laws (statutes) may be found on pages 162 to 164.

It is really a case of using legal and ethical argument to contest the validity and legality of the council's claims for the individual's assets.

MAKING A REFUND CLAIM

A list of the information that should be provided in a claim to the local Primary Care Trust is provided on pages 162 to 165. The claim form should be completed and sent to the Chief Executive of the Primary Care Trust in which the person in care lived. When sending the claim form ask for confirmation of safe receipt. The Primary Care Trust should also supply a further consent form for signature. This is to enable the Primary Care Trust to obtain confidential social and medical information from social services and the patients G.P. as part of their investigation.

The claim process may take a considerable time to be investigated by the Primary Care Trust and may take more than 12 months. If there is a long delay consider lodging a complaint with the Ombudsman or Healthcare Commission. Common excuses for delay are that the G.P has not supplied requested information or the person dealing with the claim is off sick or on holiday.

If the claim to the Primary Care Trust is unsuccessful then an appeal should be lodged with the Primary Care Trust or if directed by the Primary Care Trust in their refusal letter direct to the Strategic Area Health Authority at the address supplied.

If that is also unsuccessful a formal complaint may be lodged with the Health Service Ombudsman for cases of individuals in care prior to April 2004 and to the

Healthcare Commission for cases after 2004. The procedural details are supplied by the Primary Care Trust at each stage in the process.

When a claim is lodged and accepted there is also the possibility that the claim is accepted only in part. In other words someone may have been in care for several years but the refund is accepted for only the last 12 months or so. In this event it is suggested that the complaints/appeal procedure again be followed. Any evidence of health at the cut off date will be invaluable and should be supplied as part of the appeal process.

There is no reason why the refund due for the accepted period plus interest should not be paid by the Primary Care Trust during the appeal process. Do not however sign anything which states that the payment is made in full and final settlement of the claim.

The personnel at Primary Care Trusts and Strategic Health Authorities who are involved with fee refund claims and appeal procedures are unlikely to have any legal qualifications and legal experience. The result is that any legal arguments put forward at this stage are ignored on the grounds that they are matters more properly dealt with by the Courts or the Ombudsman/Healthcare Commission.

When the "Review Panel" is arranged the claimant is invited to attend. Such invitations are likely to specifically exclude the attendance of a professional adviser. This should be challenged as it a basic legal right to have some form of representation (legal or otherwise) if desired. This should be used as part of the complaint to the Ombudsman/Healthcare Commission.

The representative of the person in care may wish to appoint his legal representative as Attorney to attend on his behalf. This however is also likely to be refused by the Strategic Area Health Authority.

Local Citizens Advice Bureau offices, Law Centres and Age Concern Offices may be able to provide free assistance or at least be able suggest someone who is able to assist further.

It should be borne in mind that PCT's do not pay any professional costs of anyone assisting in the claim. Professional Assistance may however be available on a no win no fee basis or from a law centre.

Preliminary legal advice may be obtainable free of charge from a firm who holds an appropriate Community Legal Service franchise.

Other forms of Legal Assistance may be available. Many household insurance policies provide legal cover to pay legal costs. Also membership of a Trade Union or consumer association may provide legal assistance.

General - Part 2

For those who wish to minimise or totally avoid the loss of assets in the payment of care charges

This section deals with the positive steps which can be taken and also which legal and ethical arguments can be used to avoid having to use assets to pay care fees.

When it comes to the payment of care fees there are three points to consider:-

A)   The Protection of Existing Capital Assets.

And

B)   The Protection of Income.

And

C)   The Protection of Future Assets.

The most important starting point in any action to protect assets is that many more options exist where there are two people as in the case of a couple as opposed to an individual living alone.

Introduction to the problem.......

An average residential care home placement is likely to cost at least £300.00 per week in the North of England. The cost of a Nursing Home placement is likely to exceed £400.00 per week. The costs for care in the South of England are significantly higher.

If the individual "in care" has sufficient income to cover the weekly care charge then the loss of capital will not arise. Most people however do not have the benefit of a weekly net income of £300.00 to £400.00 even if they were to sell their house and invest the proceeds to generate further income. Those in care who are treated by the council as self funding will still be entitled to their Attendance Allowance and perhaps a contribution from the local Primary Care Trust in respect of any health care component of their care package. A financial contribution for personal care is not paid for those in England and Wales. Care funding arrangements are however different in Scotland, Wales and Northern Ireland.

If income is insufficient then capital is at risk as it will be sought to top up the fees. The more capital is depleted the lower the resultant income. When capital falls to £21,000 (the figure for 2006/07) the local council then make payment of the fees subject to a contribution of £1.00 per week for each £250.00 of capital held over the lower threshold figure of £12,750. The individual's income will also be sought to reduce further the amount of contribution payable by the council. When capital falls below £12,750 a further assessment means that the council make payment of the balance of the home fees again subject to any assessed income contribution.

The payment of £1.00 per week means that for every £1,000 between £12,750 and £21,000 a contribution of £4.00 per week is required. If the person remains in care long enough then his capital will fall to £12,750 as his capital will not produce a net income in excess of 20%. This is of course because £1.00 per week out of £250.00 totals £52.00 for the year.

The individual is permitted to retain a modest amount of "pocket money" of £19.60 per week for personal needs and expenses (for the year 2006/07).

A). PROTECTION OF CAPITAL ASSETS

The list below provides a summary of the main options that are available to challenge an assessment or allegation by the Council that capital assets are to be taken into account for the purposes of calculating the amount(s) which the individual must pay towards their care costs.

The topics covered are in alphabetical order and therefore do not infer that any option is stronger or superior to another. Also the available options may not be suitable in a particular case when all factors are taken into account. The main purpose of the list is to show the wide range of possibilities to refute council demands. In addition the list demonstrates the merit of taking independent legal advice from a qualified and experienced lawyer who specialises in the field of asset protection/law for the elderly. Most law firms describe this area of the law as "Private Client". As a result a small firm which does not have a "Private Client" department is unlikely to have someone sufficiently specialised, experienced, qualified and knowledgeable to be able to deal with asset protection cases involving care home fees. Indeed it is not uncommon for those who enquire of a law firm what can be done to avoid the use of assets to pay care fees to be told nothing can be done.

In terms of the options available what may be relevant to a person in care aged 65 will be different to someone in care who is aged 95. Life expectancy will therefore also play a significant part in choosing the correct options.

Other options may also exist and so once again the benefit of seeking advice from someone who is familiar with council assessment procedures is likely to be helpful.

One word of caution however is that so far as possible seek a lawyer who will use the law to argue points in your favour and not a lawyer who is just an "administrator" who recites what the law is and is therefore unable or unwilling to explore or challenge boundaries or depart from "the system". In seeking a lawyer think of the lawyer as a white collar tradesman. In everyday life one would not consider employing a "tradesman". In reality one would seek the services of a specialist whether a builder, an electrician, a plumber, a joiner, a plasterer or some other defined specialist who only does one type of trade. Lawyers are just the same, and a specialist is likely to be the more helpful and knowledgeable than a lawyer on the high street who deals with many types of legal matter. A specialist is also more likely to have the experience and confidence to challenge a local council and or Primary Care Trust.

For a representative such as an Executor, Attorney or Receiver any costs involved would be payable from the estate of the deceased/donor/patient as the case may be. Some law firms operate free legal clinics.

As the health of a person in care can change significantly

during a brief period do not be afraid to seek updated advice or indeed ask for a further NHS eligibility assessment to be arranged. Also the law develops with new cases being considered by the Courts. As a result a weak position one day may improve the next.

Further Health Service Ombudsman cases and decisions by the Healthcare Commission will also affect what arguments are used.

Options:-

The following legal arguments are for use in challenging a local council and or a Primary Care Trust over their refusal to provide full care funding.

1]. **ABUSE OF POWER**

Cases do exist concerning the frustration by a public body of a legitimate expectation. In other words where a person is led to believe something as reality then it would be wrong to deny that belief or withhold what has been reasonably expected.

Councils and Primary Care Trusts are public bodies. A person who requires care due to ill-health and or frailty and who has paid Taxes and National Insurance Contributions would therefore expect any required level of care to be provided free of charge as part of the NHS. The refusal to provide such care free by the local Primary Care Trust could therefore be said to amount to an abuse of power. The failure of the Council in their conduct of their needs assessment to either recognise this or refuse to actively assist the person requiring care to obtain NHS funding could therefore also be said to represent to an abuse of Power. This abuse largely arises as the Council find it easier to charge the person in care and they do not understand the legality of the subject of charging people for care.

The reality of the situation, especially in terms of identified cases of wrongful charging is that when such a case is identified a refund is duly made to the wrongfully charged person.

The question arises just how far does this refund go? In many cases an individual will be assessed as having to contribute towards the care costs from income only because the amount of capital held is below the lower threshold amount (£12,750 for the year 2006/07).

As a result the balance of the care fees will be paid by the local council.

It must then follow that the contribution paid by the council will exceed the contribution made by the individual. In practice however it is the policy of the Primary Care Trust not to refund the council's contribution. It also seems to be the case that it is not the policy of councils to seek refunds from the Primary Care Trust.

One would have thought that the Council would have been duty bound to recover any money wrongfully paid. In contrast councils are quick to say that they are obliged to obtain refunds of care fees and other monies such as rent or council tax arrears from individuals and indeed are prepared to take people to court even for relatively small amounts as in the case of council tax arrears.

Furthermore, the duty on the Council in order to properly represent and preserve the financial interests of the public would suggest that they should seek to instigate formal action against not only the Primary Care Trust but also government for the whole business of charging people for their care.

As to "abuse" in general it is worthy of note that "abuse" is defined by Action on Elder Abuse as: "A single or repeated act or lack of appropriate action, occurring within any relationship where there is an expectation of trust, which causes harm or distress to an older person".

The forcible extraction of life savings and pension income easily falls within this definition.

2]. **AFFORDABILITY**

The usual excuse given by government for failing to provide full funding for all those who require care is that it would cost too much.

If this is true then it is difficult to comprehend how a civilised country cannot afford to cover the costs of care for the elderly and disabled but can afford:-

(a) To involve itself and its citizens in open ended ongoing wars in numerous trouble spots around the globe?

(b) To provide a minimum sum of £250.00 for newly born babies who have never contributed to the system and will not do so for at least 16 years?

(c) To fund huge numbers seeking Asylum and then neglect to deport those whose applications fail?

(d) To write off massive amounts of third world debt?

Several further pertinent questions of financial mismanagement also arise such as:-

(e) What has happened to all the taxation revenue received from oil companies and also again from the motorist?

(f) What has happened to the huge amounts

(g)   paid by telecom companies for mobile telephone licenses?

(g)   Perhaps most significantly how can membership of a club called the European Union be affordable when politicians owe their first duty to the welfare of citizens of the United Kingdom as their elected representatives?

Sadly the sick and the vulnerable continue to be taken advantage of as they are not in a position to challenge the blatant unfairness of the system and the financial abuses directed against them.

3].   ANNUITY

Rather than an outright gift of an asset consider giving the asset (whether it is a property, a share in a property, stocks and shares or money in a bank or building society account) in return for a periodic monthly sum. The payment each month would act as an annuity where the sum paid can either remain the same or increase each year. The agreement could contain provisions that it is to continue for a certain period of time or until a certain event takes place such as the recipient of the annuity no longer lives at a designated property. Caution will be needed to avoid the payment from being treated as taxable income. The agreement could therefore be phrased as being the payment of capital in periodic instalments with perhaps additional payments to recompense for loss of interest. This could then be said to represent the use of the capital gains tax allowance of the giver. The gifting of cash would be an ideal possibility if the recipient required a capital lump sum to assist in the purchase of a property.

The agreement could also include provision that the recipient would maintain any property thus reducing the responsibility of the giver.

A return of capital calculated as being a maximum of 6% per year should be sufficient to avoid income tax difficulties.

4]. BUSINESS INTERESTS

The council are likely to seek the value of a business for the payment of care fees. The variety of businesses and business types that are available and the complexity of business taxation laws in general merit the taking of detailed legal advice. The main asset of a family business which is a limited company is likely to be the shares in the company. If such shares are still held by a person who is in poor health and so may envisage future care the advice required would be the timing and overall implications concerning the transfer of shares to other family members.

Where one spouse is or has been in business then the ownership of domestic assets such as the family home should be checked as the house may have been transferred into the name of the other spouse to protect it against loss as a result of business failure. If this is the case then a further transfer should be considered.

5]. **CARE FEE INSURANCE**

It is possible to take out an insurance policy to provide an income to pay care fees. If care fees were say £375.00 per week then an annual income after tax of £19,500 would be needed. A policy to provide such an amount is likely to be expensive. However a policy to provide the full amount would not be needed as other income would reduce this. First of all a state pension of only £80.00 per week would provide over £4,000 thus reducing the policy requirement to £15,500. Other occupational pension income and income from the investment of property sale proceeds would provide additional funds. Any care component will also add £2080 per year for those on the low band, £4316 per year for those on the medium band and £6916 per year for those on the high band.

Attendance Allowance would also reduce the

balance required from a policy. The higher rate of weekly attendance allowance of £62.25 would produce a further £3237 per year.

If the policy premiums were an investment that provided a lump sum on death because no money was required for care fees then the level of premium would be much higher.

6). **CARER IN OCCUPATION OF PROPERTY**

When a carer is still in occupation of a property the value of the property should be treated as an asset not available for the payment of care costs. (See also Constructive/Resulting Trusts below).

Where possible therefore a younger member of the family such as an adult grandchild could move in and use a spare bedroom. A son or daughter who owned their own home would not be in a strong position unless he or she had sold their own home to move in with the parent to provide the required care.

7]. **CONFLICT OF INTEREST**

Any decision by a council could be challenged on the basis of a conflict of interest as they have a legal duty to arrange and pay care fees in the first instance. Furthermore matters are even more suspicious given the fact that many council's seek to ascertain personal and confidential financial details before any care assessment has been made to determine the actual level of health care required. Despite a lack of entitlement to such information the council may also seek personal financial information of a spouse. Such information should not be divulged.

A formal complaint should be lodged with the council when any such information is requested on the basis that such a request is an abuse of power (see above) and is information to which they are not entitled.

8). CONSTRUCTIVE/RESULTING TRUSTS

Where one or more children still live at home as carer(s) the value of the property should be disregarded. The person at home may also provide services such as assistance with washing and dressing, cleaning, shopping or work for free or for a low wage for a family business. The carer is in an especially strong position if they are unable to work due to the level of care being provided, in terms of hours worked. The position is even stronger if they have also contributed to the housing costs such as purchase monies, mortgage instalments and or repair and maintenance costs.

(see also Proprietary Estoppel below.)

It may also be that during a couple's lifetime they ultimately agree to dispose of the house to certain people. Therefore it can be argued that the surviving spouse received the total interest in the asset in reliance of and on the understanding that it would indeed be passed to the mutually agreed beneficiary(s) by the survivor. As a result there is a prior obligation which takes priority over care fee payments as the Property is held on a resulting trust or an implied trust for the mutually agreed third party.

It follows that it is unreasonable for the wishes of the previous deceased owner to be frustrated. The deceased owner relied upon his expectation that future care costs were not an issue as such fees are covered as part of the National Health Service. The argument here is also stronger if the deceased died before 1993 and so would be unaware of the shift in care home funding from central taxation to local taxation.

9]. **COUNCIL HOUSE PURCHASE**

If a council tenant purchases his or her property with the financial assistance of others (mostly adult children as an investment) by the provision of capital purchase money and or the payment of mortgage instalments then for the long term protection of the "beneficiaries" a formal Declaration of Trust should be entered into by all parties. This provides evidence of the agreement and the true beneficial ownership of the property. The person who holds the beneficial ownership is the person who is actually entitled to the sale proceeds of the property. The person named on the deeds has merely the legal ownership which has a nil value as the value of the property exists in the beneficial (or equitable) ownership. For an explanation of equitable ownership see Proprietary Estoppel below. See also miscellaneous matters point M) below.

For the additional protection of the beneficiaries it would also be advisable for the Will of the buyer as legal owner to state that the property is to pass to the beneficiaries in accordance with the declaration of trust. (See Precedent Number 2 below for an example of the suggested wording for inclusion in a will). An Enduring Power of Attorney to deal with future mental incapacity would also be advisable as it would enable the property to be transferred or sold without delay.

Beneficiaries should also bear in mind that the rules of purchase mean that the Property would need to be held for a period of several years to avoid having to repay all or part of the permitted discount from the original purchase price.

10]. COURTS

See Litigation below

Also consider the alternative to formal court action of "Alternative Dispute Resolution". This is a mediation service and can be used to resolve the matter without the delay and expense of formal court proceedings.

Further information on this can be found on the government website:-

www.civiljusticecouncil.gov.uk

Also local directories will have a section on providers of mediation services.

11]. DECLARATION OF TRUST

See Council House Purchase. Such a document is of vital importance as it represents the actual written evidence that the interest in a property claimed by a person who is not a legal owner actually exists.

The legal basis and purpose of this document can be found in Section 53 (1) of the Law of Property Act 1925 which provides that "a declaration of Trust respecting any land or interest therein must be manifested and proved by some writing' signed by the settler or by his will.

The settler is the legal owner of the property in question but the written document confirms that despite this he is not the person entitled to the sale proceeds. He is in effect holding the property in his name as a Trustee for others, usually the person(s) who provided the purchase money or the person(s) paying the mortgage.

12]. DISCLAIMER

The case of Townson v Tickell from 1819 is proof that an individual who is a beneficiary of a gift under an estate cannot be forced to accept the gift.

Therefore say a husband owns in his sole name the matrimonial home. He then dies and the house on the face of it passes to his widow under his will or under intestacy law.

In this case the house, if it was transferred to the widow it would be at risk in the payment of care fees should the widow require some form of future care.

The widow to keep her options open could simply leave the house in her late husband's name. The option then exists for her to make a disclaimer at some future point (evidenced in writing) to the effect that she does not wish to inherit the house.

This situation itself is perhaps old fashioned but does still arise today. It is most frequently found where a couple marry before 1970 and the bride was under the age of 21 at the time of the property purchase. At that time a person was not an adult until 21 and so could not hold property or obtain a mortgage. Section 1 of the Family Law Reform Act of 1969 reduced the age of majority from 21 to 18.

As a result when the age of majority was 21 the house would have had to be bought in the sole name of the husband if he was the only one over 21. Even if the couple have moved since then the new house may again have been bought in the husband's sole name. Lenders in the past took a dim view of married women as they were likely to stay at home or give up work to bring up children and so would not have an income to assist in the payment of mortgage costs.

This old fashioned situation is of tremendous assistance for asset protection purposes as it means that the widow is able to live in a property free of charge which is not legally hers.

The widow if faced with the possibility of care in future could then disclaim her entitlement to the house. If the house is transferred to the widow it would no longer be possible to disclaim it. In this case the Variation option as detailed below would need to be considered.

If disclaimed the house would then pass to the next blood relative(s) under the Intestacy Rules if there is no will or to the next person(s) entitled under the will.

From a legal perspective the effect of a Disclaimer is that the beneficiary i.e. the widow is treated as if she had died first. In other words the replacement beneficiaries say the children inherit the property from their father's estate rather than receiving a gift from their mother.

Where possible this option should be used in preference to a Deed of Variation. This is because the person signing a Disclaimer has no control over who is next entitled whereas a Deed of Variation enables the asset to be directed to the person(s) nominated by the beneficiary. It is therefore better for the property to pass elsewhere by operation of law rather than at the request of the widow. The professional costs involved in the preparation of a deed of variation will far exceed the costs of a disclaimer.

The above actions may also have an effect upon the Inheritance Tax position of the surviving spouse and so legal advice is essential. If the subject of Inheritance Tax is an issue then a Deed of Variation would be more appropriate with such Deed including extensive discretionary trust powers and provisions.

13]. **DIVORCE**

If the matrimonial home is owned by the spouse in care but occupied by the other spouse then failing to act would place the whole value of the house at risk if the spouse in care was the survivor.

If the spouse in care still has mental capacity then it may still be possible to transfer the house into the name of the spouse at home or transfer the house into joint names as tenants in common and create a will trust to protect the house. (see below regarding wills).

If this is not possible then the spouse at home could seek a divorce and an order of the court that the house (or at least half of it) be given to him or her thus protecting part or all of the house if the spouse in care was to be the survivor.

If in this example the house was transferred into the sole name of the spouse remaining at home then the house would again be at risk should that person ultimately require care.

A transfer of the property into the joint names of one or both spouses plus the children could be considered as an alternative. The personal circumstances of the children would need to be fully considered to avoid other future problems such as the death, divorce, redundancy or bankruptcy of the son or daughter.

The attitude of both parties is also relevant because the ownership of an asset by someone unwilling to challenge a claim for care costs would put the asset at greater risk than someone with strong feelings of injustice who would actively dispute any claim on their assets to pay care costs.

14]. EQUITY RELEASE

In many cases this option will be considered only as a last resort. It is however also very useful for Inheritance Tax planning purposes. Present schemes are far better than the original schemes due to increased competition amongst financial service providers. Most of the modern schemes operate as types of mortgage where a capital sum is released. The procedure is essentially the same as a mortgage application with additional formalities to ensure that the applicant and their potential beneficiaries and/or family understand the implications. The capital sum which is provided by a lender can then be spent (or gifted with caution). The interest that accrues on the capital debt can be added to the loaned amount increasing the debt until it is redeemed. Alternatively if there is a desire to prevent the debt increasing the interest can be paid in the normal way perhaps by the beneficiary(s) of the capital sum.

This is especially helpful if children use the capital to reduce their own mortgages and so use their excess income to pay the parents mortgage. This payment would also give the children an arguable proprietary interest in the property. (see proprietary estoppel below).

The funds released in this way are lump sum based but schemes also exist that provide a monthly income. The monthly income method is unlikely to be of assistance in asset protection as income is likely to be taxed. Also both the income and the capital remaining in the property would be at risk.

Equity release schemes are probably more likely to be of interest to those who have no family and who wish to benefit from the capital tied up in their homes. Modern schemes are more flexible as it is still possible to move house and benefit from growth in the property value.

These "equity release" arrangements are also now known as lifetime mortgages in that they allow asset rich but cash poor individuals to benefit from the value otherwise locked up in their property.

15). FREEHOLD/LEASEHOLD PROPERTY

If the property owned and at risk is Leasehold in nature consider the purchase of the Freehold by the intended beneficiaries. A freehold title is superior to a Leasehold title. A Leasehold title can also be surrendered or merged with the Freehold. The Leasehold title is therefore a depreciating asset. The shorter the period left on the lease the more attractive this option will be.

When a property is to be sold a Freehold title is far more attractive to a prospective purchaser than a mere Leasehold title even if the Lease is very long.

Newly built properties are usually sold with only a Leasehold interest. This is to enable the developers to retain control of the estate as they are able to enforce covenants on the owners of the properties as they as the Freehold owners have the better title. In due course Leaseholders may be given the opportunity to purchase the freehold interest. There will in any case be the right to seek an extension to the Lease.

This option will not be relevant or appropriate for some properties. For example in the North of England many properties especially terraced homes are in the form of a ground floor flat and a first floor flat. In order that the respective occupiers of both flats are able to ensure that they are not unduly troubled by any undesirable activities of their very close neighbours above or below, each flat has two titles. The occupier of a flat is sold a Leasehold interest in his flat but also given the Freehold interest in the other flat. His close neighbour has the same arrangement of the Leasehold interest in the flat he occupies but the Freehold in his neighbours flat. Again the purpose of this is to make it easier to keep a neighbour in order because he has the better title of being the Landlord of the neighbour. No actual money changes hands however by way of rent as the title deeds would refer to the rent as being one peppercorn.

The best approach to protect the value in the Leasehold property is therefore for the intended beneficiaries of the Leasehold property to provide the purchase money to buy the freehold interest.

16]. FUNERAL PLANS

A pre-paid funeral will assist. Say someone with £23,000 is admitted to care. The upper threshold figure of £21,000 means that the excess £2,000 would be taken to pay fees as the person would be treated as self funding. Such an amount would only last a few weeks.

Now say an average funeral bill was £2,000. If the £2,000 is used to pay for a pre-paid funeral plan the capital would be reduced to the threshold figure immediately. The individual would then qualify for council funding much earlier. In due course the beneficiaries would benefit from the full amount of money held as they would not suffer a reduction in their entitlement because of the funeral account as it had already been paid.

Some pre-paid funeral plans however are not really pre-paid in that they amount to merely an interim payment which is then deducted from the final funeral bill. The pre-paid plan may not include disbursements such as crematorium fees, doctor's fees and newspapers notices.

17]. **HEALTHCARE COMMISSION**

In cases of dissatisfaction following a refusal by a Primary Care Trust to pay for care or refund care fees already paid it is worth completing a complaint form and sending it to the Healthcare Commission. The address and other contact details of the Commission are provided in the letter from the Primary Care Trust in their letter refusing the claim.

Before the Commission will investigate all other complaints procedures have to be followed such as an appeal to the Area Strategic Health Authority.

The time that the person was first admitted to care is also relevant as the Parliamentary and Health Service Ombudsman deals with the cases of those who were admitted to care prior to April 2004.

18]. HOME CARE

Rather than admittance to residential or nursing care the option exists for care at home. If this is considered as inappropriate or unsuitable by social services or the hospital due to the level of health care required then this is evidence in support of a claim for full NHS funding. See also the Malcolm Pointon case below.

Care at home may involve an application to the council for a grant to adapt the home to be suitable for a disabled person such as a downstairs bathroom or a downstairs bedroom.

However such applications may be means tested.

19]. HUMAN RIGHTS ACT 1998

There are various Articles in the Act which may be used as valid arguments that it is unlawful or wrongful for money belonging to a person in care to be taken to pay his care costs. These Articles are best used in addition to other technical arguments rather than on their own.

The Human Rights Act itself is substantial in scope and so only a brief summary of the most relevant articles are described below:-

(A) **ARTICLE 1 of the First Protocol**

This states that every natural person is entitled to the peaceful enjoyment of his possessions. No one shall be deprived of his possessions except in the public interest and subject to conditions provided for by the general principles of international law.

The term "possessions", in the context of the Act, includes interests in land, shares, and the value of a business. The taking of the assets of an individual because they suffer from poor health could not possibly be said to be in the public interest. Indeed the opposite would be the more accurate statement especially if society is truly civilised.

(B) ARTICLE 3

This relates to Degrading Treatment. Conduct will be degrading when it is such to arouse in its victims feelings of fear, anguish and inferiority capable of humiliating and debasing them and possibly breaking their physical or moral resistance.

The requisite humiliation can be in the eyes of others or the individual himself. This therefore includes those who are suffering from some form of mental incapacity and the family of the individual in care.

It is not unreasonable to suggest that those who are told they must pay towards their care will be very unhappy and probably angry and upset as in practice it means that the sooner they die the less it will cost the beneficiaries of their estate.

Visits to the care home by those beneficiaries are likely to be uncomfortable to the extent that visits are less frequent than they would otherwise have been.

Also the majority of residents in the same care home are likely to be funded by the council at least in part. Therefore if the law correctly says that the lower permitted amount is only £12,750 then that must logically be what society says a life or a lifetime of work is worth. The next question is therefore by what right is government whether local or national able to determine a value for a working life. Taking the argument further it could also be said that a working life has no value because those who have never worked and therefore have no or very little capital are not required to pay.

(C) **ARTICLE 5**

This deals with the right to Liberty and Security. Whilst the Liberty part of this article refers to those detained in prison the position of a person in care is not dissimilar if he is placed in care for his own safety or the safety of others and is consequently prevented from continuing to enjoy an independent and private lifestyle. It may also be the case that he is in care against his will.

In terms of Security the elderly frequently find great comfort and security in the assets which they have saved and worked for over their lifetime as it is their legacy to pass on to future generations especially in these times of high property prices and education costs. The introduction of university fees means that more and more grandparents are anxious to contribute what they can to avoid the grandchild from accruing debt and or to assist in preventing the grandchild from having to seek paid employment to supplement their meagre student income.

(D) **ARTICLE 7**

Whilst this article refers to criminal law it is still of relevance as it refers to the confiscation of assets. The taking of assets to pay care fees can therefore be considered as confiscation and is also pertinent as it is punitive as those who do not have assets do not suffer a similar financial penalty.

This article is therefore of relevance as assets are being confiscated despite the fact that no criminal offence of any kind has been committed or even alleged. The "offence" that has incurred the "fine" is therefore being old, unwell, disabled or a terminal illness which has necessitated society in the guise of the local council to intervene and arrange alternative "suitable" and safe accommodation.

(E)   **ARTICLE 8**

This article relates to respect for private and family life.

As a result this article of the Human Rights Act is arguably the most relevant and helpful.

Article 8 aims to protect individuals from interference with the right to private and family life, the home and correspondence.

The scope for challenge to Council assessments using Article 8 manifests itself in various ways:-

(a)   The habit of Councils to demand to see financial records sometimes going back several years.
(b)   The ending of family life in terms of being prevented from spending money as desired e.g. gifts.
(c)   The refusal of the assessed person to return to his own home.
(d)   The prevention of the individual from living with his spouse or partner.
(e)   The taking of property sale proceeds traps the individual in care as he is

unable to return home at a future point if his health improves. The loss of capital to pay fees combined with an increase in property prices would in many cases make it difficult to get back on the property ladder.

(f) The invasive nature of the questioning by council financial assessment officers for details of all assets and income and also the financial affairs of a spouse. One question frequently asked is whether the person has a will. There is no possible justification to ask such a question as it is not only cruel and insensitive but it is totally irrelevant and of no business to the council.

(g) The abuse of power/conflict of interest by council officials in not suggesting that independent legal advice be obtained.

(h) The lack of assistance by the Council in actively seeking NHS funding and challenging the NHS when funding is refused.

(i) The failure of the council to ask about debts and other claims and obligations that the assessed person may have and which are payable in priority to any council demands.

(F) **ARTICLE 14**

This deals with the prohibition of Discrimination. The present system discriminates in several ways. Those in other parts of the United Kingdom do not suffer such a large financial penalty when admitted to care. The eligibility criteria used by the authorities to decide who and who is not entitled to funding from the NHS also differs from county to county. Those with similar health conditions even in the same care home can be treated differently. Those who have little assets even if they have squandered such assets are rewarded for such behaviour whilst those who have saved are punished.

Most importantly where English Law conflicts with European law then European law prevails. This means that the Human Rights legislation takes precedence over domestic English law.

20]. **INVESTMENT**

When an individual has significant assets the subject of paying for care will be less of a worry if that individual has sufficient income to enable payment of the monthly care fees without having to resort to capital.

Those with poor performing assets and or a property would be able to increase their income to pay care fees on investing property sale proceeds.

The length of time that such fees are to be paid will also determine the level of concern. Someone in care aged 65 will need to take into account capital growth to provide for future increases in care fees whilst someone aged 95 will be less concerned with future care fee levels.

The advice of an independent financial adviser is also likely to be of assistance to advise on what financial products are available to produce tax free income and or allow the capital to grow whilst taking tax free withdrawals of capital. Financial advice will also be available to highlight what life insurance based investments are available which are disregarded for the purposes of care home fee assessments.

If there is a low return of income from a trust fund, reinvestment should be considered to increase the income if the increased income would allow the capital to remain intact or the investment strategy revised altogether in an effort to seek capital growth, avoiding income and thus reducing the income available for the payment of care fees.

It should also be remembered that Councils have no right to dictate how a person should invest his or her capital.

If a Trustee has any difficulty he may wish to consider retiring and appointing a replacement.

21]. **JOINT BANK ACCOUNT**

This option is of assistance where an account is held in joint names. If say Mr X received an Inheritance of £50,000 and placed this in a joint account with his wife then for assessment purposes even though the money really belonged to Mr X he would be assessed as if one half of it belonged to Mrs X. Similarly if Mrs X withdrew her apparent £25,000 from the account the balance on that joint account would then be only £25,000 for assessment purposes.

On the other hand if say Mrs X had the Inheritance and put her husband's name on the account then she could in theory lose half of it to pay for her husbands care fees as the council would treat it as being a joint matrimonial asset.

The general principle that applies therefore is to ensure as far as possible that the person who is to enter care has as little money as possible in their name both solely and jointly.

This may involve the closure of accounts. If accounts are closed it is safer to make withdrawals by cash rather than obtain a closing cheque as this would represent a link to the original account. For safety purposes whilst more time consuming it would be preferable to make regular cash withdrawals.

The taking of regular cash withdrawals is also helpful as such withdrawals then form part of the regular household expenditure.

If a family member is an authorised signatory to an account this does not make it a joint account.

22]. **JOINT FREEHOLD/LEASEHOLD PROPERTY**

See below under Palfrey case and also Wills Generally.

23]. **LICENCE**

This topic relates to the situation where a person occupies a property belonging to another. The most common legal arrangement for this would be a lease or other formal tenancy. If say an owner of a property gave his property away he may request a lease from the beneficiary. Leases are fine but are rather formal and complicated. As an alternative the beneficiary of the property may grant a licence to live in or use the property. The main advantage of a license is that it can be revoked at any time.

The gifting of property in this manner is fraught with other potential serious problems especially in view of the planned new pre-owned assets rules and the possible liability to an income tax charge based on the rental value of the benefit in using the property.

Further taxation difficulties may arise as a result of Capital Gains Tax primarily the loss of the sole or main residence exemption.

A short term but formal agreement such as a shorthold tenancy agreement lasting 12 months is likely to be a safer option which can be renewed every 6 or 12 months if needed. Renewal would however require the agreement of both parties.

24]. **LIFE POLICIES**

For the purposes of contributing towards care fees the value of any life insurance policies should be ignored. The encashment proceeds of any policies would however be at risk. Care therefore needs to be taken in any financial re-organisation.

When considering the investment of capital money it would be worth seeking advice from an independent financial adviser who can advise not only on potential returns but also on which policies would likely qualify as being unavailable to pay care fees.

Some types of investment also enable a tax free income to be taken. These types of investment can be useful in their own right as a source of tax free income.

The payment of monthly premiums for a life policy should also be disregarded in any income assessment.

Where permissible consider writing life policies in trust if that has not already been done. Also it may be that the premiums for the policy have been paid by another. In this case the person who pays the premiums has an equitable claim to the encashment proceeds.

Alternatively it may be possible for the benefit of the policy to be assigned to another.

25]. LIFETIME GIFTS (a)

Many people wrongly believe that giving assets

away before admittance to care will avoid the problem altogether. The most common example is where a property is transferred into the names of the children. This does not provide a solution to the problem as the gift would probably be treated by the council as an attempt to avoid care fees. The gift would therefore be disregarded. This means that the value of the gifted property would still be taken into account as an asset and thus available for the payment of care fees. The greater the amount of time that has passed since the gift was made however the more likely this option will prove successful. The reason for this is that if someone gifts a house when they are in good health it is more difficult for the council to argue that the transfer was made simply to avoid future care charges.

It should however be remembered that the gifting of ones home in this way may result in other serious problems. Difficulties could arise if the original owner fell out with the recipient or if the beneficiary died first, divorced, was made bankrupt or redundant. It is also possible that a Capital Gains Tax liability would arise on a sale of the property if the beneficiary had other property.

This option is also likely to prove costly as a result of new Tax rules which affect those who apparently give assets away but continue to use the assets. The cost would be an income tax charge based on the market value of the benefit used. The effect is different if after the gift is made a market rent is also paid to the original property owner. The payment of only a nominal rent would not therefore solve the problem.

As regards care home fees however if some other reason can be given to explain the apparent gift then there should be no problem. Perhaps the most common example would be the transfer of a Council House to children after the relevant discount refund period had expired on the basis that the children had paid the purchase price and or mortgage and or property improvement costs.

Another valid argument for the gifting of property would be to give peace of mind to the children should a parent re-marry.

Please also see Declarations of Trust and Council House Purchase sections above.

26]. **LIFETIME GIFTS (b)**

A safer option to Lifetime Gifts (a) may be to transfer the property into the joint names of the owner(s) and the children. If this is contemplated please see above under Joint Property.

A word of caution is that when a second name is added to an asset whether it be a property as a beneficial joint tenant or a bank account then on death that account would pass to the survivor. This may not be in accordance with the long term wishes of the original owner of the property or asset.

In practice the fewer the number of beneficiaries the more flexible this option will be. This is because fewer people will need to agree to a sale. The transfer of assets by a parent into the joint names of himself and an only child would result in the least difficulty.

Where assets pass to a surviving joint owner it is still possible for the surviving owner to re-direct the joint share that has passed to him. See the section below on Variations.

If the change in ownership relates to a property then it should be borne in mind that if the property is unregistered land (In other words there is no record of the property at the District Land Registry because it has not changed ownership since registration was compulsory for that area or the type of the last transaction) any new transfer would then have to be registered. Any privacy held would then be lost as the names of the new owners would be available for public inspection from the land registry records including the purchase price or nature of the other "consideration". The consideration is what each side to an agreement give or promise the other party to the agreement as their part of the deal or arrangement.

27]. **LIMITATION ACT 1980**

This act details the time limits for the commencement of any legal claim. Different types of legal claim have different time limits. For matters concerning Contract and Tort this is 6 years from the time when the existence of the claim was known or should have been known.

A matter concerning Contract arises where two or more parties enter into an agreement. The agreement may be made in writing or may be verbal.

A matter concerning Tort relates to a civil wrong or injury arising out of an act or a failure to act for which an action for damages may be brought. Such matters are independent of any contractual relationship.

Therefore if a contractual dispute with the council continues for more than six years then they are unable to take any action to recover any sums claimed as they would be statute barred. This means that the court would not even entertain hearing a case as the council have left it too long to take any action. The subject of Negligence as detained below falls under the tort category.

The issue of a failure to act (or negligence to be more precise) may be directed towards a council who fails to identify that an individual is entitled to some form of NHS funding.

28]. LITIGATION

This term is used to describe the attempt to settle a dispute involving a court. This should be viewed as a last resort when all else fails. It is commonly termed as Court action. There are two sides to any court action. One party is the plaintiff and he is the person bringing the claim to court. The other party is the defendant and he is the person who is defending the claim. In terms of nursing care matters it would be unlikely that a person would seek to bring an action against a Council and or a Primary Care Trust as the issue of cost would be prohibitive. The financial resources available to Councils and Primary Care Trusts would be limitless in comparison to the individual. Ironically if the individual has no such fears of cost then he does not have a problem anyway as it would mean that he had enough assets or resources to fund his care fees.

It would be more likely that a claim would be brought against an individual for assessed unpaid care fees. This is likely to involve smaller sums (unless the council allow debt to accumulate over a long period) and so the question for the person in care (or more likely their representative) would be whether to defend the claim or not. If the money was to disappear anyway in the payment of the care fees then there may not be any risk in seeking to challenge the claim.

The threat of litigation is often merely just that, a threat without any true intention of taking matters further. This is not unreasonable from the view of the council as most people threatened with formal action pay up to avoid it even if they dispute the claim. In many cases especially for small sums it is unlikely that any formal court action would arise as the costs and time involved could not be justified. It is also unlikely that a council would wish to take the risk of creating a dangerous precedent for such a small sum if the case was lost as it would also mean that sums taken from others in similar circumstances would need to be refunded.

If the representative acted under the Authority of an Enduring Power of Attorney or as a Receiver then it would be more probable that the Council in their efforts to extract money would lodge a complaint with the Public Guardianship Office.

This may be very helpful in that it may force the Public Guardianship Office to do something to assist. The function of the Public Guardianship Office is to protect and preserve the assets of the person in care. As a result it is difficult to see how the Public Guardianship Office could demand that any fees are paid without question. A person who receives such a communication from the Public Guardianship Office should refer to those arguments listed in this book (and the issues raised in the Coughlan judgement) which are relevant and ask for the Courts assistance in defending against the improper demands of the council.

Interestingly Lord Scarman said in one case:-

"I must make clear my view that the principle of fairness has an important place in law......and that in an appropriate case it is a ground on which the court can intervene to quash a decision made by a public officer or authority in purported exercise of a power conferred by law".

The request to the Public Guardianship Office would be to support the refusal to pay care costs. In refund claims it would also be worth asking the court to assist with the making of an order that the assessed care fees be refunded. When a person has died the Public Guardianship Office are unlikely to be of any assistance as their authority ceases on the death and so the court no longer has jurisdiction at this point.

If there is any dissatisfaction with the Court's assistance or because of a lack of assistance after a death then consider refusing to pay any court fees claimed on the basis that the court have failed in their duty to assist in the preservation of the individuals assets. Consider also the lodging of a complaint with the Court and or your Member of Parliament.

Assistance with legal costs may however be available through the Legal Services Commission or as part of a legal expenses insurance policy. Some household policies include such provisions.

See also Courts above in regard to Alternative Dispute Resolution.

29]. MP (Member of Parliament)

A letter to an MP to complain in the strongest terms how outrageous it is to be charged for care may be helpful only if to register the level of anger felt. Several points in addition to the points listed at "Affordability" above could be raised in such correspondence. The first is to ask why the recommendations by several Royal Commissions that care home fees should be funded by central taxation have not been implemented. A second question is to enquire of the personal view of the MP on the subject. If the MP does not agree with you then how is he able to represent his constituents properly as his personal views conflict with the majority of those he purports to represent. A third point where the MP is of the party in government is to ask why the manifesto commitment to take action on the subject has not been honoured.

It may also be helpful to write to your local councillor. This will be especially so if he has ambitions to further his or her political career in parliament itself.

It may also prove interesting to solicit the assistance or views of your local member of the European Parliament. Such a person is likely to have several researchers who may provide useful arguments especially in view of the Human Rights Act.

In the event of any dissatisfaction consider lodging a complaint with the Parliamentary Ombudsman.

30]. MARRIAGE

a). If an unmarried couple live together and

one goes into care the value of a one half share of the jointly owned property may be taken into account by the council for the assessed contribution towards the care costs. If therefore the couple married then the whole value of the house would be excluded (if the person remaining in the home was aged over 60). If however the other partner acted as carer the value of the property should be totally disregarded.

b). Under Section 42 of the National Assistance Act 1948 one spouse is liable to maintain the other. Therefore if one spouse is admitted to care he already has a pre-existing legal duty to maintain his spouse who is still at home. As a consequence it can be seen that there are no funds available to pay care fees. The income of the spouse at home takes priority in that there should be no reduction in the standard of living of the spouse at home. Some councils use this law to suggest that the spouse at home is in fact liable to use their income to pay for the spouse in care. This is incorrect. The Council have no powers even to require the spouse to provide financial details of their own savings and investments. Also a spouse at home should not be requested to make payment of anything they cannot reasonably afford. Therefore even assuming that the council's claim for a contribution was valid then any payment by the spouse at home would be unreasonable on the basis that he or she cannot be expected to suffer a reduction in their own standard of living simply because the health of their spouse no longer enables them to reside and be cared for at home.

In reality the expenditure by the spouse at home is likely to increase because he or she will have the added expense of travel to visit their partner and also their income will have been reduced due to the withdrawal of attendance allowance. The spouse will also probably take confectionary, reading materials and other sundry items.

As a result of the Civil Partnership Act 2004 civil partners enjoy the same legal rights and protection as a spouse.

Un-married partners should also use the same arguments as certainly from a discrimination point of view the law now makes little noticeable distinction to couples who are married or not and the un-married partner is still a dependant.

31]. **MEDICAL NEGLIGENCE**

Where a person requires care of any level as a result of medical negligence then it is the Health Authority which is responsible for the medical negligence and consequently they who it should be argued is liable to fund any care arrangements. To argue otherwise would be to financially reward the party guilty of the negligence. (See also Negligence in general below)

32]. **MENTAL HEALTH ACT 1983**

If a person is in care pursuant to the Mental Health Act then he or she should not be charged any care fees on discharge to a private care home.

The main Section of relevance here is Section 117 of the 1983 Act which states that those discharged for aftercare after being sectioned are entitled to accommodation without charge.

33]. **MOVE HOUSE**

If a property owner lived in his home which was worth say £200,000 he could sell his house and move to a smaller property costing say £100,000. The excess £100,000 could then be gifted with the result that the new property effectively hides the gift. The gift of course may not be a gift as it may be to satisfy some other interest such as a trust or proprietary estoppel (see below).

Another twist on this theme would be to move to another country where relatives lived e.g. Scotland as their fee charging regime is significantly less harsh.

The sale of a property at below market value could be challenged however. If a lower value was being paid because of expenditure (i.e. Proprietary estoppel) by the buyer this would be an acceptable explanation.

The move to a property which required capital expenditure would also provide the opportunity for the ultimate intended beneficiaries to acquire an interest such as proprietary estoppel.

Another possibility using the same principle would be to sell the property and move into rented accommodation to allow sufficient time to dispose of all the property sale proceeds by gift.

If the move was to a newly built property then it should be remembered that the principle of Proprietary estoppel will not be of much assistance as a newly built property will not require repair and maintenance for quite some time. Expenditure such as decoration, buildings insurance and annual maintenance charges for the common areas could be paid by the ultimate intended beneficiary as this would be of future assistance.

Receipts for all expenditure, cheque book stubs, and bank statements should be retained.

34]. NHS FUNDING CLAIM

Where any degree of Health Care is required always consider lodging a formal claim to the local Primary Care Trust for full NHS funding. At the very least the whole process takes such a long time that the delay may enable other avoidance measures to be implemented. Before a claim is lodged ask the Primary Care Trust and or Social Services for a copy of the NHS funding eligibility criteria assessment which was conducted before the person was admitted to care. With the passage of time new Ombudsman and Healthcare Commission cases may be published which assist further.

The subject of NHS funding is also of great relevance to anyone in care who has been discharged under the Mental Health Act 1983. (see above).

If on enquiry it is found that no eligibility

assessment has been conducted ask why this is the position and ask for one to be done immediately.

Independent evidence of poor health should also be obtained from the individuals G.P. if it is suspected that the individual suffers from some form of condition e.g. one or more of the forms of dementia which would enable full funding to be obtained. The medical advice thus obtained is likely to be only a letter from the G.P. but its content could be very valuable as it may refer to a terminal illness or the type of dementia suffered by the patient. The cost for this will vary but would be money well spent.

In any eligibility assessment do not assume that the criteria that have been used by the PCT and or the Council are correct. Also if someone requires care resist any attempts to classify needs as being social. The term "Social" is a smokescreen to distract from the true situation that a person in care is there because of the state of their health alone. The simple tasks of washing and eating are not social matters. Not eating results in weakness and eventually death. Not being able to wash results in discomfort and possibly illnesses. Some people in care are so immobile that they can only be moved using a hoist.

35]. NATIONAL HEALTH SERVICE AND COMMUNITY CARE ACT 1990

This Act which came into force in April 1993 altered the care fee regime to its most significant extent for many years.

Before then funding for residential nursing home care had largely been met by central taxation in the form of social security income support. After this date such funding became the direct responsibility of local councils.

Oddly this Act is not the one usually referred to by Councils in their claims. The most likely reference will be to the National Assistance Act 1948. The response to this is of course that it has been superseded by numerous other statutes and case law. This Act should therefore be viewed as a distraction from the full position. The full position includes the numerous and varied other statutes which apply and the cases that have been decided by the Courts and the decisions of the Health Service Ombudsman and the Healthcare Commission.

The argument is that this act does not allow individuals to be charged for their care as it has been superseded by other laws. Also reference can be made to the unjustness of the law itself.

Section 44 (2) of the Act is interesting as the wording states that "…..where a person is provided with accommodation under this part of this Act the local authority providing the accommodation shall recover from him the amount of the payment which he is liable to make".

Two points arise. The first is that this can be interpreted as saying that the law does not say that a person is liable to pay care costs it says that a person has to pay costs for which he is liable As liability is disputed then nothing need be paid. The individual in effect does not accept liability especially if he is incapacitated.   If there is incapacity how can there be any agreement to pay any sums.

Secondly due to the closure of many council run care homes the care is not provided by the council any longer. It is instead provided by private care homes. Therefore the council have not provided the care and so do not have authority to charge for services provided by others.

Also councils have a legal duty in any event to make such arrangements as are necessary for care and to fund such care costs. Also if there is a liability to pay for the provision of care how is it possible that only those who have assets are deemed liable? This is something of a contradiction at the very least.

36]. NEGLIGENCE (General)

Negligence is one of those words which is often misunderstood. The word negligence is usually believed to relate to a situation in which someone suffers some form of loss because of the failure of another to act. Whilst this is true Negligence in fact may also occur where someone does act when he should have done so.

If a claim for negligence were therefore made against a Council for their assessment that a person had to pay for their care this could be said to be negligent as the Council is under a duty to make a proper assessment. The position of the Council is to say the least precarious, as they have a conflict of interest. On the one hand they seek to determine how much an individual has to pay them but at the same time the Council have the legal responsibility to pay the shortfall.

The assessment that an individual has to make a payment for care could thus be argued as a breach of duty by the Council. If for example the council did not inform the assessed person (or their representative) of their right to independent legal advice this could be said to be negligent and an abuse of power.

In practice from a legal standpoint to be successful in a claim for negligence four points need to be proved.

(i) That a duty of care was owed. This exists because the Council are in a position of trust and vulnerable people (whether the person being assessed or his family/representative) trust that the Councils actions are not only correct but also in the interests of the person being assessed and their representative – especially if that person is the spouse.
(ii) That duty was breached. This is obviously so if care fees have been taken that were not properly chargeable. A refund of wrongfully charged care fees would be evidence of an incorrect (or non existent) assessment.
(iii) That the individual suffered damage. Again this is so because the taking of money reduces the amount of money held by the person in care and furthermore reduces the standard of living of a spouse. He/she suffers a loss of income because the household income has been reduced to pay the other's care costs. The damage will be greater if a house has been sold to pay care fees and if that property has increased substantially in value after the date of sale.
(iv) That damage has occurred as a result of the

breach of duty. Again this is true not only in financial terms but also in the emotional damage and stress that the individual in care and his/her spouse/partner may have suffered. The health of the person in care and or a spouse may also have suffered in that the person may only have agreed to be admitted to care as it was the last resort as the priority was to preserve as much of the capital and income assets as possible.

In addition to the above the long term effects are damaging to society because it discourages individuals from saving for their retirement. The loss of money would also cause mental stress and upset. This in turn is more likely to lead to mental incapacity and so more people require care because of the strong feelings of being cheated by the system after decades of paying direct and indirect taxes when those who have perhaps never worked or have squandered their money receive care without any financial penalty. This often gives rise to unhappiness and strong feelings of resentment where those in care who pay for everything see and interact with those who have everything paid without query or question.

The negligence itself could equally be said to be a breach of Trust. In this regard the law demands much higher standards of professionals than from the layman. Also ignorance of the law by the

Council or PCT is not a valid defence.

37). ONE SPOUSE SURVIVING BUT DEEDS TO HOUSE STILL SHOW BOTH NAMES

Where a surviving spouse is left at home it is worth checking the title deeds. It may be that the deeds still show the deceased spouse's name. In this case a document called a Deed of Variation can be entered into to split the title in the property in half to protect the late spouse's half. The Variation could include a gift to the children from the deceased parent although that would be risky in numerous respects. It would be safer to include a trust in the Variation to allow the surviving spouse to continue to use the half share of the house belonging to the late spouse. If the deed is entered into within two years of the death of the first spouse this provides better protection.

If the house is found to be in the sole name of the deceased spouse, a transfer into the name of the surviving spouse should only be done if there is a necessary legal or financial reason to do so.

The Variation option is available whether or not the first spouse leaves a will. This option should also be compared with the alternative of a Deed of Disclaimer (see above).

Legal advice should be obtained if the value of the property and the other assets of both spouses combined exceeds the Inheritance Tax nil rate band threshold amount (For the year 2006/2007 this figure is £285,000.) This is because Inheritance Tax becomes relevant and a more complicated Deed of Variation including a Discretionary Trust would be needed. The provisions of such a Variation would include a full list of what the Trustees are allowed to do including the power to transfer the property to the surviving spouse on a loan basis, the loan to be repaid from the surviving spouse's estate.

38). **PALFREY CASE**

The full name of the case is Chief Adjudication Officer v Palfrey (1995).

This case can be used to argue that the share of an asset which is jointly owned has no or little value for care home fees assessment purposes if the other joint owner refuses to sell it. The joint owner in care is therefore unable to release his or her share if the other joint owner refuses to sell and so no money is available at that time and until sale to pay any fees or indeed anything else. The greater the number of joint owners then the less the value as more people would need to agree to a sale to enable money to be released.

Further argument as to the valuation of the share of a jointly owned property is provided by The Trusts of Land and Appointment of Trustees Act 1996. See Further below page 126.

39]. PENSION FUNDS

For the purposes of Inheritance Tax, pension funds are usually held by Trustees in a Discretionary Trust. The main reason for this is that on the death of the pension payer before retirement the capital value of the pension fund does not get added to the value of his estate for tax purposes. Even a modest pension fund of say £100,000 would suffer a loss of £40,000 (being 40% Tax) if the deceased's estate was already in excess of the Inheritance tax threshold on death (£285,000 for the year 2006/07).

As a result the pension payer would normally be invited by the Pension Fund provider to complete a Nomination form or an Expression of wish form to set out in the event of death where and to whom the Trustees are to pay the capital or other pension benefits.

This however would give rise to three main potential problems if the capital was paid to the surviving spouse.

(a) The sum of £100,000 would be at risk if the surviving spouse re-married.
(b) The lump sum would use up part of the surviving spouse's Inheritance Tax threshold.
(c) The spouse would have a large amount of capital which would be at risk from being taken to pay care fees.

All three problems can be solved if the Nomination or Expression of wish form requested that the lump sum be paid to separate Trustees to hold in a separate Discretionary Trust rather than being payable direct to the spouse.

The same type of arrangement could be used for death in Service benefits and the proceeds of life insurance policies.

Indeed the treatment of those who have provided for their retirement raises the question of whether saving for retirement is actually a good idea at all.

It is without a doubt that the saving of only small amounts in a pension would have a negative effect as the amount of the future pension income would be less than could be gained from state benefits.

40]. PERSONAL INJURY

Where any form of care is required as a result of injury sustained in an accident the insurers of the offending party should be called to account for such care costs as part of the overall claim process. Legal advice should therefore be obtained as to the protection of any compensation award with the use of Personal Injury Trusts.

The recovery of damages may also involve having to refund sums received by way of state benefit. This should therefore be considered when deciding whether or not to accept any offer.

41]. POINTON CASE

This case was investigated by the Health Service Ombudsman in 2004. Mr Malcolm Pointon suffered from terminal-stage dementia that could hardly be more severe. As a result he met the criteria for fully funded NHS care. All his care was related to health needs as they all arose from his brain disease. The difference in this case was that Mr Pointon was being cared for at home by his wife. The local Primary Care Trust had originally argued that they could only provide NHS funded care in a nursing home setting. During the Ombudsman's investigations the Health Authority unexpectedly agreed to fund the weekly care costs of £1,000 which was equivalent to the cost of a hospital bed.

This case should therefore be used to lodge a claim with the local Primary Care Trust for funding to assist with care costs of persons who are cared for at home. These cases are likely to be rare and only arise when a spouse at home still has a sufficiently high level of health (and usually other family support) to be able to provide 24 hour care.

The provision of such funding would enable the person to be cared for in respite at periodic intervals to give a spouse and other family carers a break. This would also render any questions from the Council on the assets owned by the person in receipt of the care as irrelevant and unnessary.

42). PROMISSORY ESTOPPEL

This technical principle came to prominence with the decision in the case of Central London Property Trust Ltd. v High Trees House Ltd. [1947] K.B. 130 The case is interesting and due to its importance and usefulness in care home fee avoidance it is explained in detail below:-

This should not be confused with Proprietary estoppel which is also considered below. It is however very similar in nature.

The facts of the case are that in September 1939, the plaintiffs Central London Property Trust leased a block of flats to the defendants High Trees House at an annual rent of £2,500. In January 1940, the plaintiffs agreed in writing to reduce the rent to £1,250, plainly because of war conditions. The war was to blame for a large number of vacancies in the flats. No express time limit for the operation of this reduction was set. From 1940 to 1945 the reduced annual rent of £1,250 was paid. In 1945 the flats were all occupied once again. To test a principle the claim by the plaintiffs was that High Trees House should pay the full rent of £2,500 for the last two quarters of 1945. This was successful because the war had ended. The most important point however is that the judge also said that had the action included a claim for arrears for 1940 to 1945 then the agreement in 1940 would have operated to defeat the plaintiffs claim. This is interesting because there was no consideration for the plaintiff's promise to reduce the rent. (The term consideration is considered in detail below under Proprietary Estoppel).

It follows that this case may be cited to show that a claim by the Council for care fees is contrary to case law. At first sight it is not quite clear how the High Trees House case is relevant to care home fees.

The main beneficiaries of the High Trees case are those who were of voting age before 1948. This is the time that saw the enactment of laws creating the welfare state. The public in return for the creation of the Welfare State accepted increased and additional taxes and also National Insurance contributions. It follows that it is now too late for Society in whatever form be they national or local government to seek to force people to pay for health care when this was the whole point of the additional payment towards the welfare state.

The doctrine of estoppel shows that if one person makes to another a clear and unambiguous representation of fact intending the other to act on it, if the representation turns out to be untrue, and if the person does act upon it to his prejudice, the representor is prevented or "estopped" from denying its truth.

The present modern so called free and capitalistic system mirrors the High Trees House Principle as people are encouraged to work hard to create personal wealth. Whilst that wealth is taxed in a number of ways (both direct and indirect) it is a fact that the net income may be spent and applied at the total discretion of the owner.

It is therefore unacceptable for a person who chooses to save and invest his money to be punished severely for doing so. The person has relied on the assurances that his net income was his free of taxes. To tax it again cannot be acceptable as otherwise there is no reason to save for retirement or make provision for ones family in the event of death or illness.

It is as if someone who pays income tax at the basic rate of 22% then had a further 18% taken at the end of the tax year to make him a higher rate tax payer if he had not spent his already taxed income.

Those working and paying taxes after 1948 also have the same argument as the provision of health care via the National Health Service free at the point of delivery and when needed is expected without further charge. The means testing for care provision amounts to double taxation.

43]. PROPERTY IN SOLE NAME OF ONE SPOUSE

Where both spouses live in their matrimonial home but the deeds are in the sole name of one spouse and that spouse is the elder and especially a man, consideration should be given to that person making a will to include a trust. The terms of the trust would be to allow the surviving spouse to live in the house for as long as they wished. If the survivor required care then the full value of the house would be protected as it would not be an asset owned by the surviving spouse.

The trust can take one of several forms. For present purposes the two main alternatives are Life Interest Trusts and Discretionary Trusts. A third type of trust is a right of residence.

A common example of a right of residence trust would be to allow a child to continue living in the family home for several years until he arranged his own accommodation or whilst he was still engaged in full time education. Similarly a trust may be to allow a second spouse to live in the matrimonial home until they remarry again or co-habit. This is probably rather harsh in these times and could be challenged by a surviving spouse.

A Life Interest trust in a will would specify that the surviving spouse had the right to continue to live in the house for as long as they wished. Additional provisions are also usually included to allow the surviving spouse to sell the house and use the money to buy a replacement property. Also the life interest means that the spouse is the beneficiary of the value of the trust rather than just the property. Therefore the trust would allow the property to be sold and the sale proceeds invested to produce an income that would enable the surviving spouse to pay rent in say sheltered accommodation.

A discretionary trust is considerably more complicated and legal advice should be taken if this is contemplated. This is likely to be the better option if the value of the house is more than the Inheritance Tax threshold figure (£285,000 for 2006/2007) or because the next in line beneficiaries say the children have a problem such as a pending divorce or they already have assets close to or in excess of the Inheritance Tax threshold figure.

If the younger person owns the house then consideration should be given to a transfer of the house into the name of the elder person or into joint names as tenants in common. The joint names option would be to protect at least one half of the house. The Tenants in Common type of ownership is important because this means that the share owned by an owner on death forms part of his estate. The opposite type of joint ownership is called a beneficial joint tenancy. This means that on the death of a joint owner his share passes to the other joint owners automatically. This latter and usual way of holding property (especially domestic residential property) by a couple demonstrates why so many properties are at risk because the survivor becomes the sole owner automatically.

Similarly, regardless of the respective ages of the

couple the house could be transferred into the name of the person whose health was poorest on the assumption that he or she will die first and so the full value of the house could be protected using the will trust method.

When considering this option and the ages of the respective parties remember the statistical difference in life expectancy between men and women is on average 6 years longer for women.

Specific legal advice should always be obtained on the subject of discretionary trusts from an experienced qualified lawyer. A large number of developments have occurred in the field of Tax planning during the last few years and more changes are due to take effect. It should always be remembered that tax law changes on a yearly basis.

44). PROPRIETARY ESTOPPEL

This is arguably the most useful option in that it can be used by the vast majority of property owners. The older the property, the more useful this option is likely to be. This option is a combination of technical principles from Land Law and Contract Law.

To understand this concept one must first

understand a basic principle of Land Law. Land Law is the area of law, which governs legal ownership and other rights, duties and interests over land and property.

There are two aspects to consider. The legal position of property ownership and entitlement can be thought of in the same way as an iceberg.

An iceberg has two parts, the visible part above the water and the other much larger part hidden below the surface.

Land Law can be thought of in the same way as an iceberg in that a property has an obvious visible part and an underlying invisible part. The visible parts are called legal interests. They are visible as they are evidenced in writing. Such interests would be where someone owns the freehold title or a leasehold interest allowing the tenant to use the property for a fixed period of time. In this case the person's legal position would be evidenced by the title deeds (or land registry title information document) in their name.

Land Law also involves equitable interests. Again in simple terms these interests are like the lower part of the iceberg in that they are not readily visible. Equitable interests are owned or claimed by third parties who do not own the land and whose claim is not readily visible from the deeds or the circumstances in general.

Proprietary Estoppel can be described as a legal situation where a third party is encouraged by the owner of a property to spend money on the property. In return for this expenditure there is an agreement or expectation that the property or some interest in it will become theirs at some future point. The law of equity (or reasonableness) then dictates that such a person should be protected. This usually means that an attempt to pass the property elsewhere would fail. The person or persons who have the Estoppel may thus claim the property or their interest in it in priority to other claims.

The principle behind the estoppel is to create a prior claim to the value of the property. As another example consider the position of a person who is admitted to care but still has an outstanding mortgage. When the property is sold the sale proceeds must first be used to discharge the mortgage. If the owner in care had a property which was sold for say £150,000 but £130,000 was the mortgage then the balance of £20,000 is the amount belonging to the owner. The council can not claim any of the £130,000 mortgage money as this is payable elsewhere and does not belong to the owner.

The principle can be used to protect assets for the

intended beneficiaries as it means that if say a parent makes a gift of money to his children and the children are then encouraged to spend that money on the property it can be seen that the children then have a claim to the Estoppel. In other words the value in the property is effectively transferred from the legal interest to the equitable interest or the Estoppel.

In the long term this can then be used to defend a claim for the house sale proceeds to be used to pay care fees as the Estoppel comes first in the list of claims. Detailed records should be kept by those who spend money on the property such as retaining copies of all cheques, bank statements, cheque book stubs and also any receipts for work done on the property. Subject to the circumstances the whole situation may be evidenced further by the use of a declaration of trust setting out who has paid what and when and what interest they will receive in return. This Declaration of Trust document is especially useful if not essential in the case of a council house purchase (See above). This is because the tenant of the property who buys is the person who is entitled to the discount.

The agreement situation is also relevant in terms of the Contract Law aspect. For any agreement to be binding in law several essential legal requirements are necessary.

Of the various essential requirements one of the most important in terms of nursing home fee avoidance is "consideration". The consideration is what each party to the agreement gives to the other as part of the agreement. To be more precise the consideration can either be money or monies worth. Very few contracts involve each party giving the other money. Perhaps the change of money from sterling to Euros or Dollars for a foreign trip would be the most likely example.

The "monies worth" usually involves one party giving money in return for a material possession of the other or perhaps the provision of labour in the form of some type of service.

The legal definition of what is valid consideration goes on to say that this consideration must be real but it need not be adequate.

In other words if say an agreement was reached to sell a vehicle to a friend for £1,000 but in reality the true value was £2,000 this difference in figures would not prejudice the contract. The agreement would still be legally valid and binding on both parties.

When applied to proprietary estoppel this means that if someone spends money on a property it is not that important how much is actually spent.

The important point is the actual act of spending money. It follows that if a house (or a share in a house) was worth say £150,000 but the children as the intended beneficiaries spent say only a couple of thousand pounds then in theory this should be sufficient to protect the whole value of £150,000.

Certainly the more that is spent then the stronger the future legal argument. If money is to be gifted to children it would also be helpful if such money was gifted as smaller amounts on a regular basis and by cash.

In many cases children also provide unpaid care and other services. This should also be used to protect a house as this "labour" could also be classed as "consideration". See also Constructive Trusts above.

When a property is gifted to a son or daughter it may be that no money is given in return. To be valid there must be some consideration. In this case the agreement detailing the gift will therefore contain words along the lines of "In consideration of the natural love and affection by the parents for their son/daughter". This is also accepted as a valid form of consideration.

If there is a transfer to the children where no money is given then it is advisable that the transfer documentation formally states that the consideration is the proprietary estoppel owned by the children. The main reason for this is because all documents sent to the Land Registry are available for public inspection. The council would therefore be able to obtain a copy of the transfer deed. If the deed recites the existence of the proprietary estoppel this is evidence that it is not a gift to avoid care fees.

Although the existence of the estoppel differs from a mortgage on a property the end result is much the same. If a person enters care and has a property with a mortgage then on a sale of the property the lender has first claim to be repaid the amount of the mortgage.

If children use their money to discharge any remaining money outstanding on a mortgage this also gives them a strong claim.

When a person holds a proprietary estoppel he too has first claim to the sale proceeds.

A typical scenario of a proprietary estoppel case which comes before a court is where one person owns a property in his or her sole name. In time that person meets someone who moves in to their home. They are encouraged to spend their money by contributing to the mortgage payments and or paying for repairs and improvements. When the relationship breaks down the owner of the property throws the other out. The position of the thrown out party is recognised by the court and they are compensated to the amount of their contribution bearing in mind the increased value of the property and the value of the property before any expenditure was incurred. The Court therefore "stops" the owner of the property from taking advantage of the other by not repaying the contribution made on the expected basis.

Due to the usefulness of this option also in terms of its application to Inheritance Tax planning and Capital Gains Tax planning a further explanation and information is detailed below.

45]. PUBLIC GUARDIANSHIP OFFICE

The Public Guardianship Office in London have overall legal jurisdiction for those individuals who do not have sufficient mental capacity to enable them to deal with their own property and affairs.

This involves situations where someone has to apply to the Court to be appointed a Receiver for the mentally incapacitated person. This person is appointed by the court and acts as directed by the court.

Alternatively this procedure is not required if the mentally incapacitated person has granted a valid

Enduring Power of Attorney. In this case the person or person appointed as Attorney(s) have a duty to apply to the Court for registration of the Power if and when mental capacity is considered to be in doubt.

If a claim for a refund of care fees involves the argument that the person is mentally incapable then a first step before lodging a refund claim is to actually register the Power with the Court as otherwise this would contradict the basis for the refund claim.

If you act under the authority of an Enduring Power of Attorney or act as Receiver for a mentally incapacitated person write to the Public Guardianship Office and ask for their assistance in challenging a claim for care fees. Also if there is the possibility that fees have been wrongly charged ask the Court for their assistance in obtaining a refund.

The amount to which the Court will assist is likely to be minimal or non existent but it at least provides formal evidence of the efforts made.

This may also prove of assistance in case a complaint is made to the Court for your failure to pay invoiced care fees. If the court are unwilling to assist in challenging a council it is equally likely that the Court will not assist a council in obtaining the patients money.

This will also delay matters giving additional time to investigate and implement other asset protection measures.

Do not be put off by a complaint to the Public Guardianship Office by a Council that you have not paid care fees. The obtaining of medical evidence in support of the claim for NHS funding due to poor health should be obtained at the earliest opportunity. Further support in the form of legal advice would also be of assistance in correspondence with the Public Guardianship Office.

46]. PUBLIC INTEREST/PUBLIC POLICY

There is an argument that the charging of care fees is unlawful as Members of Parliament are the servants of the public not the masters. There have been several Royal Commission reports and other studies which have recommended to Government that the fees charged for care should be funded from central taxation. This is also a top priority of the public as evidenced by the Health of the Nation television poll in 2005.

Also the elected labour government had promised on several occasions to deal with the unfair charging of care fees but have failed to honour such commitments.

In April 2005 the Health Committee also published a report into NHS Continuing Care eligibility criteria. The report detailed the present post code lottery and the unfairness of the system.

47]. REFUSAL

There is also the option to blankly refuse to provide any information to the Council so as to prevent them from conducting their financial assessment. Bear in mind council powers to register a caution at the Land Registry against a property. This option is therefore really only useful if assets are not property based or the property has little or no equity value because for example the whole value would be needed to repay a mortgage and or other debts.

If this approach was adopted the Council are likely to assume that assets over the threshold amount are held. However this would not entitle the council to avoid their legal duty to arrange and pay for whatever care was determined as being necessary.

If the age or level of health of the person in care is such that life expectancy is short then refusal as part of an ongoing delaying process may be sufficient to resolve the problem. A brief life expectancy will also be evidence that the individual should be fully funded by the NHS because of a terminal condition.

If this option is used also bear in mind that on death a formal Grant of Representation may be required to enable the assets to be collected in. This would mean that the Council would be able to discover in due course the size of the estate and who was responsible for the administration of the estate. To try and avoid this problem assets would need to be disposed of as lifetime gifts or the assets placed into the joint names of the owner and intended long term beneficiaries so that they pass by survivorship and thus avoid the need for probate.

From the administration of the estate point of view a Grant of Representation is almost always needed if an asset exceeds £5,000 in value. One of the most troublesome assets to deal with is a shareholding. The problem is that a formal Grant may be required to deal with the disposal of shares worth even very modest amounts.

If a grant is not obtained it is vital to consider the wording of any declarations required by asset holders as such declarations may include an indemnity. The indemnity may go so far as to say that it is also given in a personal capacity by the person claiming the asset.

48]. SCOTTISH SYSTEM

As the system in Scotland involves the payment of less fees because of different rules on payment for social care it is therefore discriminatory and thus unlawful to charge those in England and Wales more than those in Scotland. Those in England and Wales pay the same taxes and so are entitled to the same benefits.

The main difference is that the distinction between what is regarded as purely health care and what is regarded as personal care is less defined.

A move to Scotland and especially if that is where family members live is likely to prove helpful. Before any such move it would be advisable to check funding arrangements in case the local council in England and Wales are still responsible for the care costs.

See also Human Rights Act Article 14 above

49]. SEVERANCE OF JOINT TENANCY

A jointly owned property which is subject to

survivorship will pass automatically to the surviving joint owner(s). To avoid this so that on the death of one joint owner his share remains as part of his estate it is necessary to sever the joint tenancy. This changes the ownership to a tenancy in common. To be a valid severance the other joint owner(s) must be served with notice of the severance.

If there are more than two joint owners then some may hold as beneficial joint tenants and some may hold as tenants in common.

If the severance of joint tenancy is contemplated any other relevant factors should also be considered. For example if one joint owner has numerous debts it will mean that on death his estate will have a share in a property which may be liable for the payment of such debts whereas if the property passed to other joint owners by right of survivorship then there would be less likelihood that the property would have to be sold to release money to discharge the debts.

To be valid the joint owner who is served with notice does not need to acknowledge the notice. This is of course crucial where one joint owner is in care because of dementia. In this case it is also advisable for someone to sign the severance notice as a witness to confirm that the joint owner was informed of the severance.

If a married couple, although still married are separated then the subject of severing the joint tenancy may already have been considered and dealt with. Where a couple re-marry and have respective children from their previous marriages it is advisable for the jointly owned property to be held as tenants in common to ensure that the family of the first to die do not lose their inheritance as a result of a step-parent leaving it to their own children. It is vital that a will is prepared to protect the surviving spouse and respective children.

50]. SOCIAL CARE

In practice the most common excuse for a refusal by a PCT to provide NHS funding is that the person who requires care does not need nursing care but only requires social care. Indeed to distract the public the actual department name in the PCT or the local council may be called the "social care directorate" or something similar that emphasises the term "social".

The provision of nursing care and social care is such that a reasonable distinction cannot be drawn to differentiate each type of care. If someone is assessed as being in need of "social care" only then it begs the question why does such a person require 24 hour care away from their own home. If it was truly a case of "social" need then why would care in the community services not be adequate? The answer is that the level of care required goes beyond a need for mere social activities and or interaction. The amount of state funding payable for Social care in the home in the form of Attendance Allowance at the higher rate is £62.25 per week. If someone has a stroke and cannot eat then such assistance is not social it is life preserving and thus health related.

The dictionary definition of the word "social" refers to someone who prefers to live in a community rather than alone. A person in care does not choose to be in care they are there as a result of necessity. If the person suffers from dementia they may not be aware of their care environment and have probably not consented to their new living arrangements. The most obvious cases are those where one spouse is taken into care because his wife or husband is no longer able to provide the necessary level of care. Being removed from living with one's spouse or partner must surely amount to the opposite of social.

51]. SPEND MONEY

Whilst this may seem obvious the expenditure of money is often overlooked. Any money spent means less is available to pay care fees. The most common examples would be pre-paid funeral plans, vehicles (say to enable a carer to arrange trips) family holidays and personal chattels such as furniture, jewellery and antiques. It may also be that money is paid to assist younger members of the family with the payment of their private school fees or university education fees and maintenance costs. Costs for the upkeep of pets and other animals should also be taken into account.

Such expenditure is also in addition to any other outgoings such as the payment of debts in general and other regular outgoings such as covenanted gifts to charity and insurance premiums.

The values of personal chattels are not taken into account for the purposes of care home fee assessment. As a result it is theoretically possible for money to be "invested" in the purchase of antiques or other high value items. The high mark up on gold would suggest that the investment in jewellery would not be a profitable investment.

If valuable items are sold then the money realised would be at risk and so a gift of the items would be preferable. The gifted item could always be referred to as a family heirloom.

Opportunities for expenditure may also present

themselves where there is a business or where a business can be purchased.

If a property has been gifted previously, then money (capital and or income) could be used to pay a monthly amount in respect of rent. This would mean that the owner would have to disclose the income on his/her income tax return. The payment of income tax on the rent would be preferable to the payment of 100% in care fees.

In terms of spending money please remember Articles 1 and 8 of the Human Rights Act above.

52]. THEFT

The whole business of local councils charging those who require care could be suggested to amount to theft. The definition of Theft under the Theft Act 1968 is "the dishonest appropriation of property belonging to another with the intention of permanently depriving him of it".

The involvement of the police however is best avoided unless it can be shown that signatures agreeing to the payment of care fees have been forged or obtained under undue influence by a council official or other third party.

Another issue which could be considered is that of

obtaining money by deception. When an assessment is conducted and an individual and his representative are told that they must pay for care and that statement is proved to be incorrect by the payment of a refund then it is difficult to see the logic of why the charging by a council is described as merely wrongful in comparison to an individual who obtains money under false pretences. The individual would face criminal charges and penalties where in comparison councils and Primary Care Trusts suffer no penalty whatsoever and are free to repeat the "offence".

A representative of a person in care who does not hold official authority to Act such as a Power of Attorney or the Appointment as a Receiver should always proceed with caution. Serious consideration should be given as to the obtaining of this authority such as a Power of Attorney (where sufficient mental capacity still permits this) or a Receivership order.

Returning to the definition of theft it does appear that the taking of money by the council to pay care fees can be said to be dishonest as the full legal picture has not been divulged by the council to the "assessed" person or their representative and that there is an intention to permanently deprive the individual of his assets as it is to be spent on care.

53]. TRUSTS – (Generally)

Where possible argue that the asset which the Council seek to take into account for their assessment purposes does not belong to the assessed person in that it is subject to a trust.

An example of where this could be used is where one spouse has left an asset be it cash, property, shares etc to the other spouse by will on the understanding that the surviving spouse would leave it to their children and or grandchildren. Thus the property could be said to be held in Trust for the children/grandchildren as the true beneficiaries.

To prevent compliance with this trust agreement is therefore unacceptable as it would render the surviving spouse in breach of trust and thus his or her estate liable to legal action.

There are many types of trust and thus a detailed explanation of each type is beyond the scope of this book. However the most likely trust that would be evidenced would be a trust arising from a Mutual Will (see below).

54]. TRUSTS OF LAND AND APPOINTMENT OF TRUSTEES ACT 1996

Section 11 of the Act states that the Trustees of land shall in exercise of any function relating to the land consult the beneficiaries of the land who are of full age and beneficially entitled to an interest in possession of the land and so far as possible then give effect to those wishes.

This means that anyone who has an interest (or rather an entitlement to a share of the sale proceeds) in a property has the right to have his say on what amount the property is sold for and the Trustees are to comply with the beneficiaries wishes.

It must then follow that if someone with an interest in a property refuses to agree to a sale of their interest in the property then the value of the interests of other beneficiaries who are similarly entitled are unable to release their interest and thus their share of the property has no or merely a nominal value because it cannot be sold. An asset which cannot be sold can therefore be argued to be worthless at that point in time.

Any assessment for care fees is based on the value of an individual's assets at the time of assessment not on what the future value of the asset will be. However any future re-assessment would take into account the value of the asset at that time.

It should also be remembered that if a property owner is mentally incapacitated so that he is unable to dispose of his property and he has no Power of Attorney then his property is unsaleable until the appointment of a receiver takes place because no one has legal authority to be paid the sale proceeds.

In this situation if the Council have assessed that the individual is liable to fund the full cost of his care then the Council are likely to make payment of the care fees but register a land charge so that they will receive a refund of the care fees that they have paid when the property is sold.

55]. VARIATION

When a person dies their beneficiaries are entitled to their estate. Please note however that the Court has power to make changes to how an estate is distributed if a successful claim is lodged. The beneficiaries either benefit under the terms of the deceased's will or if there is no will under the Intestacy Rules. The Intestacy Rules are contained in The Administration of Estates Act 1925. Section 46 of the Act details who and to what extent the next of kin are entitled.

The case of Townson v Tickell as detailed above under Disclaimer shows that a beneficiary of a gift under an estate cannot be forced to accept the gift.

Whilst a Disclaimer may be useful the difficulty is that the original beneficiary has no control over who receives the gift in his place. The Deed of Variation however solves this problem. The Deed of Variation is also known as a Deed of Family Arrangement.

The content of a deed of variation is very similar to the content of a will. The variation explains the circumstances and states first of all who is entitled to the estate whether under the will or the Intestacy rules. The deed then goes on to say what has been agreed by all those who take an interest in the estate and who is to be a new beneficiary. The original beneficiary therefore directs their entitlement to whomever they wish.

The Deed of Variation may deal with the property and or joint bank accounts and joint shareholdings or any assets in the sole name of the deceased. The change in beneficiaries may not direct assets elsewhere but instead may modify the entitlement to include the benefit in some form of trust that the original beneficiary may use.

The Variation deed may also be used to sever a jointly owned property to put the severed part of the deceased's property back into his estate.

An example of a deed of variation can be found in the precedents section below.

56]. WILLS – (Generally)

Where a couple jointly own a property a wise option would be to sever the joint tenancy to create a tenancy in common. This is the legal way to describe the situation that each joint owners half (or other proportion) of the house forms part of their estate on death. In other words the house (or to be more precise the share owned by the deceased joint owner) does not then pass to the surviving spouse or partner or other joint owners by right of survivorship.

Both spouses/partners then make wills to say that on a first death the surviving spouse/partner may use their late spouses/partners half of the house for the rest of their life. This means that at least one half of the house would be protected from care fees. It would also serve to protect the ultimate beneficiaries if the surviving spouse/partner re-married.

This option can also be combined with the Palfrey case option and Section 11 of the Trusts of Land and Appointment of Trustees Act option as the half share of the property is not freely available for sale because the other owners i.e. the Trustees of the Will Trust and then the ultimate beneficiaries must agree to a sale. If they do not agree then the property cannot be sold and so it has no or little value.

Another asset protection combination is the use of Proprietary Estoppel (see above). When one spouse is left and particularly where the surviving spouse is female it is almost certain that the household income will fall dramatically. This provides the perfect explanation for the children's assistance in paying for maintenance and repair costs so that a surviving parent is able to enjoy their income and maintain their standard of living.

If a couple have assets which add up to more than the Inheritance Tax threshold amount (£285,000 for the year 2006/2007) then a Discretionary Trust would be more suitable for inclusion in the wills.

Consideration should always be given to the subject of Deeds of Variation and Disclaimers following a death for suitable asset protection measures. For Inheritance Tax purposes any Deed of Variation must be signed within two years of the deceased's death.

57]. **WILLS – (Mutual)**

In reality Mutual Wills are traditionally uncommon due to their perceived restrictiveness. Such a will is the same as a normal will except it involves a contractual obligation.

For example the more usual form of will might include a gift of a house or other asset by a husband to his wife. The wife as beneficiary would then be free to leave the house in her will to whoever she wished.

If the wife has children from a previous marriage then it is likely that she would leave the asset to her children. The children of the husband could do little about this.

A Mutual will would be the same but it would include an additional provision that the husband is leaving his house to his wife in consideration of her promise and agreement to then pass the house on to someone else such as his children or to share it equally between both sets of children.

The will of the wife may therefore include provisions in her will as part of the agreement with her husband that any gift to her from the husband would then go to his children.

The agreement may be more complicated in that a

property may be left to an unmarried daughter but savings and investments are to go to the son.

It follows that although the house may belong to the widow she has an obligation to ensure as best she can that the house is then left to the daughter. The argument then exists that the house is effectively being held in trust for the daughter and so the full value of the property is unavailable to pay care fees as a prior legal obligation exists.

The money is also held for the son and so it must be retained so as to avoid being in breach of the terms of the mutual will.

The same argument can be used by the surviving spouse on admittance to care in terms of her savings and investments. If her husbands will left her the money and the will included a mutual will clause then clearly that capital is held on trust for the future benefit of the intended beneficiaries. This means that the money is not available to the Council to pay care fees.

In dealings and correspondence with councils it should be remembered that as council legal departments do not write wills nor deal with the administration of estates and trusts they are likely to have very little understanding of the legal and technical issues involved. As a result they are likely to treat any such subject with suspicion.

The Council would be highly unlikely to admit to a lack of knowledge or expertise on the subject of wills, trusts and the administration of estates.

B). PROTECTION OF INCOME

The methods available for the protection of capital outlined above may also be used to protect income. Indeed the arguments when applied for income protection may be stronger or more appropriate.

By way of example suppose a person in care has capital of £10,000 and income of £5,000 per year. Assume also that he has a spouse. As the capital held is less than the lower threshold figure of £12,750 then his capital should be safe from attack. However the income would be at risk even though he has a spouse. In most cases a wife would only be in receipt of a small state pension and so would be dependant on her husband's income to pay household bills. The question is what then should the wife do to avoid being placed in serious financial difficulty. Councils in this situation when conducting the financial assessment however usually give the wife two options.

The first is that they will take all pension income and leave it to the wife to apply for income support or such other social security benefits to which she is entitled as a result of her sudden and considerable reduction in income.

The second is to take the entire state pension but only half of the husband's occupational pension leaving her with the remaining half. As the council will however take the state pension this would still leave a wife with less than half of the household income which she had before her husband's admittance to care. It is interesting that councils take the full state pension even though the husband's pension is usually higher because he has been able to work because his wife worked at home in raising the children. At the very least equity dictates that she should have an amount at least one half of the amount of their combined state pensions.

If the husband has a very small occupational pension it may be that a wife is financially better off on benefits. It is not necessarily the benefit income that is helpful but the qualification for other financial assistance as a result of the benefit. The three most significant items of expenditure are likely to be council tax, housing costs and the new costs involved in visiting her husband such as travel, sundry confectionary items and entertainment.

What if the wife does not wish to apply for state benefits? This in itself could also be considered as degrading for a person who has always paid their own way. The Articles of the Human Rights Act as detailed above are therefore brought into focus once again.

Back to the beginning:-

a). In assessing an individual, Council Social Services endeavour to take the income of the person assessed leaving them with "pocket money" of only £19.60 per week. This should be resisted not only using the same arguments as those used for

Capital but also the additional arguments of:-

(i) There may be other debts such as Credit cards, and other periodic payments. Also what of monthly gifts to charity that are paid directly from a bank account. Frequently and for tax purposes (for the charity) such payments will be made under a deed of covenant. Therefore the payment of the gift is a contractual obligation and so should be taken into account for the purposes of assessment on the simple premise that a previous financial obligation exists.

(ii) There may be other financial obligations such as assisting with the payment of private School fees/University costs for grandchildren. Special medications and or dietary requirements of either spouse may exist.

(iii) The amount of capital held is below the lower threshold figure of £12,750 (year 2006/2007) and so it is discriminatory to take money if the capital is below this amount as they are thus prevented from reaching this permitted figure when others who have this figure do not suffer further loss. State benefit rules state that unspent income is treated as capital. As a result unspent pension income should also be treated as capital until it reaches the threshold figures of £12,750 and £21,000 respectively (for the year 2006/2007).

(iv) In cases where one spouse remains at home whilst the other is in care it should be argued that as a result of a spouses duty to maintain the other (Section 42 of the National Assistance Act 1948) any pension income of the spouse in care is payable in priority to the other spouse. To do otherwise would be to punish the spouse at home and which is therefore unlawful as it is contrary to numerous Articles under the Human rights Act 1998 as outlined above.

Remember for Council tax purposes a single person discount is only 25% not 50%. Also all utility bills and property insurance costs remain the same regardless of the number of people living in the property. If the spouse at home does not drive he or she will undoubtedly have significant expenses when travel by taxi is required.

(v) There is no reason why an unmarried partner should not use the same argument if they are dependant. Same sex relationships should also use the same arguments in view of the Provisions of the

Civil Partnership Act 2004. The position of family members who share the same household should also be argued with equal force as each can be said to be dependant on the other. If people live together whatever their relationship it is highly likely that one of the advantages is the sharing of living costs.

b). The Council should be asked what legal authority enables them to assess income as being available to pay care costs in priority to other desired expenditure. The emphasis here is on the word "priority". In other words how is an unelected council employee able to dictate how a person should or should not spend his money? Such an employee is in any event supposed to be the servant of the person who requires care.

c). If money has been paid to a person in care on a loan basis then any income belonging to the person in care is first properly payable to discharge that loan. The most likely example of this would be where money was paid from a Will Trust on a loan basis rather than as an outright gift.

Will Trust provisions when properly drafted are wide and flexible. This is to allow capital payments to beneficiaries and especially to a surviving spouse. Therefore whilst the payment of money on a loan basis is more complicated than it needs to be, it does give future asset protection possibilities. Any loan agreement as with any legal arrangement should be evidenced in writing. Any further provisions for the payment of additional sums in respect of interest on the loaned amounts would require legal advice as such interest would be taxable as the income of the trust.

d). The refusal of an officially appointed representative such as an Enduring Power of Attorney to pay income in care fees is especially useful if there is a surviving spouse. In cases of doubt guidance of the Public Guardianship Office should be sought. In doing so do not be afraid to mention any relevant legal arguments.

e). The activities of Councils are such that it may be necessary to remind them that first and foremost if they say that an assessed person does not qualify for full NHS funding that they the Council have the legal duty to arrange and pay for any required care.

f). If a person with say 40 grandchildren is only allowed "pocket money" of £19.60 per week (for the year 2006/2007) and before admittance to care buys a modest birthday gift for each grandchild of £20.00 then the pocket money amount of £20.00 is clearly inadequate as that would consume £800.00 of the £1,040 total pocket money allowed for the full year.

g). An assessed person may have other periodic expenditure which if prevented may cause inconvenience or disruption to others. Two common examples would be where a person contributes to a football pools or national lottery syndicate. Also the individual may be a member of an investment club.

In regard to assets held as part of the investment club it should be argued that the share of such assets belonging to the assessed person have a nil value as such assets are not realizable unless all other members of the investment club agree to a sale. This is even more relevant if the asset in question has fallen in value since its purchase date.

h). Where income is received it may be possible to direct that income elsewhere.

A person in receipt of an occupational pension may be able to take a reduced pension in return for an enhanced pension for his spouse.

A person in receipt of income from a trust fund may be able to disclaim such income.

C). **PROTECTION OF FUTURE ASSETS**

A person who expects to benefit from an estate of say a parent should consider their own future situation and the advantages of the options detailed in Section A above concerning the protection of Capital. This may include for example asking the parent to set up a Trust in their will and or pass assets to grandchildren.

A beneficiary who finds that his bequest is more of a hindrance than a benefit may wish to consider as outlined above disclaiming such inheritance or varying it to make it more advantageous.

To be effective a disclaimer or variation must be made after the person has a legal entitlement. For example if son A signed a piece of paper to say that he disclaims (gives up) his inheritance from his mother B then if his mother B was still alive at the time he signed it there can be no valid disclaimer as A had no legal entitlement to anything at the time of disclaimer.

A similar situation will arise in future if a Building Society announces it is to convert to bank status. Any members of the Society who have signed disclaimers giving up share entitlements at the time of opening of the account will therefore surely not be bound by such document and will thus still be entitled to the share benefits. Any

purported assignment to a charitable body must logically also fail for the same reason.

PROPRIETARY ESTOPPEL AND ITS RELEVANCE TO INHERITANCE TAX PLANNING

Although Inheritance Tax planning is a different issue from Nursing Home fees this is considered further below as it highlights an additional use of the principle of proprietary estoppel and further explains how comprehensive the principle is. Furthermore any steps taken to mitigate an Inheritance Tax liability are also likely to have the similar affect of reducing the amount available to pay care charges.

The use of the estoppel can be used to reduce or avoid Inheritance Tax. As the principle is accepted by the courts then the Capital Taxes Office are also bound by the principle in their determination of an Inheritance Tax liability. The mentioning of this subject to any legal adviser or accountant that is consulted is also a useful test to ascertain the level of expertise, knowledge and understanding held by that adviser.

Putting the principle into practice:-

Say for example Mr X owns in his sole name a freehold property worth £500,000. Mr X makes a will and leaves the property to his son Y. The difficulty with this is that the Inheritance Tax allowance is currently only £285,000. (for the year 2006/2007). This means that the balance of £215,000 (ie £500,000 minus £285,000 (subject to any other allowances and relief's)) is on death chargeable to tax at the rate of 40%. Thus

£215,000 x 40% gives an Inheritance Tax liability of £86,000. The beneficiary may therefore have to sell the property to pay the tax or obtain a loan to pay the tax in order to retain the property.

To continue the theme say Mr X although he owns the house worth £500,000 still has a mortgage of £100,000 on the property. Therefore his true interest in the property (known as the equity) is £400,000. As a result for Inheritance Tax purposes the tax liability would be £400,000 minus £285,000 leaving £115,000 x 40% tax, which is £46,000. In other words Mr X does not pay tax on the gross value of the property of £500,000 as he only owns an asset worth £400,000 to him and so only £400,000 is available to his beneficiaries. Similarly if Mr X had just purchased the property for £500,000 with a 95% mortgage then his equity would only be £25,000.

Another possibility using the Proprietary Estoppel principle would be that son Y has spent £100,000 of his own money in improving the property over the years. This may have been to build an extension for him to live in. It may have been to completely update the house with a new bathroom, kitchen, rewire, windows, decoration landscape garden etc. It would therefore be unjust that the son would suffer a loss to Inheritance Tax. Therefore it can be argued that the £100,000 as a minimum should at least be deducted from the value for tax purposes. In this event the tax computation would be £500,000 less £100,000 = £400,000 less the tax allowance of £285,000 again leaving £115,000 x 40% = £46,000 tax.

The allowance of only £100,000 as stated above would however still represent unfairness to the son Y. This is because Y would not have had the money to buy another property or invest to produce an income or other capital gain. It also fails to take into account the erosion of this amount of his contribution because of inflation and the increase in market value of the property.

The cases, which have been decided by the courts, however do go further to the benefit of Y. In theory Y could claim the total value of the property. It is not known how the Capital Taxes Office (who administer and collect Inheritance Tax) would treat such a claim because of the rules regarding gifts with reservation. It would not therefore be unreasonable to suggest that the value of the Estoppel should at least be the same proportion of the value of the property on death.

Any suggestion as to a gift with reservation should be challenged as there is no gift because the title has not been transferred to anyone else. The value of the property has been obtained by the conduct of Y and the operation of the estoppel. The value or legal title in the property is still in the possession of the original owner.

The value of the property to the original owner is less than market value as it is subject to another claim.

For the Estoppel to succeed three points are essential. The first is that the son Y must prove that he has spent money on his father's property and that such expenditure was encouraged by his father. The second is that the son relied on that encouragement that the property or a share of it would some day be his. The third point to be shown is that the expenditure was to his detriment.

As a minimum, a note should be signed by father X confirming that in return for the expenditure by his son Y on his house and which he encouraged he will make a will leaving the legal title in the house to Y.

Receipts for all expenditure should also be retained in a safe place for future use as evidence of the arrangements and actual expenditure.

The names and addresses of any third parties who can verify the arrangements should also be recorded such as the contact details of builders or other tradesmen who were party or witness to discussions. Photographs and or a video of the property before and after any expenditure may also prove useful.

Ideally the will of the owner of the property which is subject to the Estoppel should also include that the interest is left to the beneficiary not as a gift but in satisfaction of the Proprietary Estoppel.

The true final position however will not really be certain until the principle as applicable for tax purposes, is tested in the courts. Previous cases on proprietary estoppel have in general proved to be very favorable to the person claiming the estoppel.

Recent cases on the subject of Proprietary Estoppel largely involve unmarried couples where one person owns a property and a partner moves in and contributes to the mortgage, property repair and maintenance costs. When the relationship ends the property owner throws the partner out. The thrown out partner then not unreasonably seeks compensation for their contribution to the property.

The existence of an estoppel is no substitute for making a will as a will should always be made to avoid future family problems or claims by other siblings who may claim a share in the property under Intestacy laws.

PROPRIETARY ESTOPPEL AND ITS RELEVANCE TO CAPITAL GAINS TAX PLANNING

The same principles can be used to reduce Capital Gains Tax bills on the basis that other persons have contributed and so they also have the use of their own Capital Gains Tax allowance. The value or gain of the actual owner for Tax purposes is therefore reduced in a similar way as if there were a mortgage or other loan on the property.

MISCELLANEOUS MATTERS

A]. AVOIDANCE

The position in regard to the avoidance of care home fees can be considered the same as that for Income Tax. On the basis that nursing home fees are just another form of taxation the principles of taxation avoidance can be applied. As a result it should be remembered that as in taxation matters avoidance is lawful whilst evasion is unlawful.

The arrangement of ones financial and legal affairs so as to reduce or avoid care fees is perfectly legal.

When it comes to the motive for any particular action if a reason can be given for either taking a particular course of action or for refusing to follow a particular path then it is difficult to see the basis upon which such an action could be challenged. This is in general the view of the courts.

B]. COMPLAINTS

Never be put off from making a complaint to an M.P., M.E.P., local councillor, the Health Service Ombudsman, the Healthcare Commission the local Primary Care Trust, the Council or anyone else who you feel has treated you badly or unfairly. The more complaints that are lodged then the sooner elderly, disabled, incapacitated and vulnerable will stop being financially punished.

C]. **CONFIDENTIALITY**

When the council and Primary Care Trust work together closely be wary of any breach of confidential information by the PCT to the council.

If any breach is believed to have occurred consider lodging a formal complaint to the Chief Executive of the Primary Care Trust concerned and or the Office of the Data Protection Registrar.

D). **COUNCILS**

Each local authority has their own procedures and so what may be a good argument in one area may not be so successful in another. This is another reason to seek local advice from someone who knows how the local council deal with care fee matters. It is also usually cheaper for the council to arrange the care placement as the amount payable by the council will be less than the amount that would be payable direct to the care home. This is because the fees charged by the care home are likely to be higher than the maximum amount which will be paid by the council.

Having said that, the rules still give a great deal of choice to a family in deciding which care home is the most suitable.

E). **CRAG**

In their correspondence local Councils frequently make repeated reference to CRAG regulations. CRAG stands for "Charging for Residential Accommodation Guide" These are cited as the legal basis upon which the Council claims to be entitled to obtain an individuals money. Possible responses to this are:-

(i) The CRAG "regulations" were issued under section 7 (1) of the Local Authority Social Services Act 1970 some 28 years before the Human Rights Act came into force. Also the CRAG regulations are not part of the law itself but are now an interpretation of the National Assistance (Assessment of Resources) Regulations 1992. Again this is well before the Human Rights Act and thus must be interpreted differently to take into account not only the Human Rights Act but also the judgments in the main two cases on this subject namely Coughlan and Grogan.

(ii) **CRAG** does not apply as it is not accepted that the individual is liable to contribute towards their care costs.

(iii) **CRAG** refers to "residential accommodation" when the accommodation actually being provided is in a nursing home environment and or the person is not merely being accommodated in that some degree of professional interaction is being supplied.

(iv) Who interpreted CRAG to mean that individuals are charged for care regardless of all other facts and circumstances and what legal authority does such person have to effectively overrule the Courts.

F). ENDURING POWERS OF ATTONREY

Regardless on what asset protection measures are put in place there is a very high probability that the granting of an Enduring Power of Attorney will be of assistance. This legal document grants to one or more persons legal authority to be able to deal with the financial affairs of someone else. It also saves a great deal of time and expense in having to apply to the Public Guardianship Office for the formal appointment of a Receiver.

One word of caution however is that of the choice of Attorney. If the Attorney also has a personal interest, for example if they have a claim to a property under an estoppel then it would be wise to include an additional attorney who was independent. This would give protection to the Attorney claiming the estoppel on the basis that there is no conflict of interest. Furthermore a joint attorney will be able to assist his co-attorney in that the joint attorney could refuse to pay care fees from assets for fear of being challenged by his co-attorney.

The granting of Enduring Powers of Attorney will no longer be possible when they are replaced by Lasting Powers of Attorney which are expected to be in place by April 2007.

The Public Guardianship Office web site contains a great deal of additional helpful information as well as relevant forms.

G]. **FOUL PLAY**

When dealing with a Local Council and a Primary Care Trust be prepared for unprofessional conduct and attempts to dissuade you from seeking and employing professional legal assistance.

H]. **FREEDOM OF INFORMATION ACT 2000**

The Freedom of Information Act 2000 came into force on 1st January 2005. This Act provides a useful opportunity to individuals seeking information that was until only recently unavailable. It may be very helpful in establishing Council and Primary Care Trust activities by asking, for example the local PCT how many claims for refunds have been lodged with them during a certain period, how many claims have been accepted, the amount of money refunded and what action they are taking to identify other cases of wrongful charging. Similarly the local council could be asked how many people in care are currently being funded by the council and how much is being paid and how much has been sought and recovered by way of refund for those who have been wrongfully charged for their care.

One other question which will provide very useful information will be how much it costs a Primary Care Trust to deal with a refund claim.

The latter question is most pertinent if someone has been in care for only a brief period as the amount claimed by way of refund may therefore be less than the amount it would cost the PCT to investigate the claim.

I). **INCOME SUPPORT/PENSION CREDIT**

Many people fall foul of Income Support/Pension Credit rules in that they continue to claim the benefit when there is no entitlement. This arises mostly in cases where the person in receipt of benefit does not spend it but instead just saves it up. Saved up benefit or indeed any unspent income is regarded as capital. When a grant has been issued by the probate office, the Recovery from Estates Office of the Department for Work and Pensions which is based in Leeds are automatically informed. Where the deceased person was on any means tested benefit the **DWP** lodge a formal claim with the personal representative of the estate as shown on the grant for refund. The personal representative is then bound by law (Section 126 Social Security Administration Act 1992) to supply the Department for Work and Pension with any and all information requested concerning the deceased's financial history. The information supplied is then used to calculate the amount of benefit overpaid. If the estate figures supplied to the **DWP** do not match with the details on the benefit claim form the **DWP** will ask for copies of banks statements and building society passbooks from the time of claim. Any old statements found with the deceased's papers should therefore be retained by personal representatives to avoid the cost and delay of obtaining duplicates.

J]. LEGAL ADVICE

In seeking legal advice do not be afraid to ask what qualifications are held by the legal adviser and how much experience they have? The broad range of legal arguments may require the involvement of several specialists within the same firm.

One interesting question in asking for advice on a refund claim matter would be to ask how many refund claims the adviser has dealt with so far and the amount of wrongfully charged care fees recovered as a result.

The above question is perhaps most relevant when instructing a firm to deal with the administration of an estate of a deceased person who was in care.

K]. MENTAL CAPACITY LAW

The law relating to Enduring Powers of Attorney will be amended considerably as a result of the Mental Capacity Act 2005. This will replace the current Enduring Power of Attorney with the Lasting Power of Attorney. Existing Enduring Powers of Attorney will remain valid.

L]. MORE TROUBLE THAN ITS WORTH

When dealing with the local council, it is not always necessary to be one hundred percent correct in any point of law or argument. The council may see you as being more trouble than it is worth to them. This is more so if the council are unfamiliar with the range of technical arguments which are thrown at them. They also have limited numbers of staff in their legal department who may also be on targets and so will not wish to engage themselves in time consuming matters.

A good indication that you are on the right track in dealings with the council is the time between letters from the council. The greater the time that passes the longer the gaps becomes between letters. This assumes that your letters are reasonably prompt.

M). **PROBATE PROCEDURES**

As a result of new probate procedures introduced in November 2004 it is now necessary in any application for a grant of probate (or Letters of Administration where there is no Will) for deaths after April 2004 for a full inventory of the extent and nature of all assets and liabilities in an estate to be disclosed to the authorities. This means that a great deal of time and expense can be saved if assets are arranged to avoid having to obtain probate. If a property is owned then a grant would be needed as part of the title. Those with more modest means can arrange for shares to be sold or put into joint names so that they pass by survivorship. Any bank or building society account is best kept below £5,000 as is any

National Savings product such as premium bonds or savings certificates. Life polices can also be written in trust so they pass outside the estate.

When completing probate forms remember to include details of all debts. This will include a reduction in the value of a property where a proprietary estoppel exists.

Furthermore if an asset is held on a constructive trust basis then that asset is not part of the deceased's estate at all and does not pass to the deceased's beneficiaries. The most common example of this arrangement would be a Council house purchase where the purchase money and or mortgage payments are paid by persons other than the legal owner of the property.

N]. **PUBLICITY**

If any interesting issues arise consider informing the local newspaper. The fear of bad publicity may be enough to ensure a faster resolution to the complaint.

Publicity may also result in other supporters coming forward. The strength in numbers principle applies and the extra moral support may also be helpful when delay causes frustration.

O]. **RE-ASSESSMENTS**

The representative of any person in care is entitled to ask for a re-assessment to be conducted at any time. This should be done at regular intervals so as to ensure that the full amount of NHS care component is being obtained especially if there has been deterioration in health since the last assessment.

Any spouse still at home may also request an assessment of his or her own needs. In this case avoid wherever possible the disclosure of financial information.

P). **REFUND CLAIM TIMING**

From an Inheritance tax planning point of view the timing of a claim is likely to be crucial especially if the individual in care is either elderly or terminally ill. If funds are available to pay any care fees, then following death a refund can be sought. The payment of the fees reduces the size of the estate for Inheritance Tax purposes as at the date of death.

Q]. **SHELTERED ACCOMODATION**

When a person for whatever reason moves from their own home to sheltered accommodation the usual action would be to sell the house and invest the net sale proceeds. The former home owner would then perhaps use the capital to pay the weekly rent on their rented accommodation.

This would be unfair to anyone who had paid for the property either by the capital purchase price and or mortgage installments and or proprietary estoppel. In this event consider the payment of the net sale proceeds to the beneficiary. This not only passes assets so that they are free from being taken to pay future care fees but it should also enable the tenant to qualify for rent allowance and or council tax benefit which would not otherwise be available. There are no issues of gifting capital to qualify for benefit as the transfer is not a gift it is the satisfaction of an estoppel and or in accordance with a trust agreement. A council house may have to be retained until the discount repayment period had expired.

R]. STRENGTH IN NUMBERS

When attending care homes, valuable information may be obtained from speaking to other visitors. It may be that other visitors especially spouses have had a successful claim or poor experiences with the council.

S]. WILLS – PROFESSIONAL EXECUTORS

In the preparation of a will it is best to avoid as far as possible the appointment of any professional person as an Executor or Trustee. The appointment of solicitors in particular as Executors is frequently made because of an incorrect assumption by the client that an Executor of a Will is unable to receive any benefit from the will. The reality is that it is a witness to the signature of a will (and or their spouse/civil partner) that is unable to benefit. Indeed having the main beneficiaries as the Executors could be very helpful in that they can proceed at their own pace and arrange matters to their own advantage if they are also the beneficiaries. The administration is also likely to be much quicker. Of course Executors must still administer the will according to the law and the terms of the will. An Executor is still free to instruct a third party to assist or deal with the administration of the estate on behalf of the Executors. All reasonable estate administration costs are payable from the estate as an Administration expense.

Where a professional person is an Executor it makes any claim for a refund of care home fees more difficult and expensive. It should not be assumed that a professional Executor will be aware of the existence of a possible refund claim.

In view of the responsibilities of Executors in general professional Executors would also be wise to consider the merits of renouncing their role so as to avoid having to deal with a refund claim. This is especially so in the case of small estates.

When a bank is appointed as an Executor further expense and delay can arise because the bank instruct lawyers to deal with the refund claim.

CARE REFUND CLAIM

Required Information for claim submission:-

1. Name of Primary Care Trust to which claim is to sent.

2. Title and name of claimant. *(ie person in care)*

3. Private Address of claimant prior to admittance to care.

4. Name and address of current/last care home.

5. Claimants Date of Birth.

6. Date of Admission to care home in 4.

7. Residence before admission to care in 4.

8. Does claimant claim future care fees. *(ie yes or no)*

9. If 8. No the reason why not. *(eg claimant died on   ).*

10. If third party acting add name address and status. ie. Executor, Administrator, Receiver, Power of Attorney, Benefits Agency Appointee, Next of Kin as the case may be.

11. Reason(s) for lodging claim.

12. Medical Conditions suffered by the claimant.

13. Medications taken by claimant. *(It is probably easier to say "Please refer to G.P. records").*

14. Name of Claimants G.P. *(This is likely to be the G.P. used by the care home).*

15. Detail correspondence address of where PCT should write in reply to claim.

16. Add any other comments relevant to claim.

17. Add summary of complaint. *(This will largely be that the claimant was wrongfully charged for care).*

The above information should for ease of reference be set out on A4 size paper.

Of points 1 to 17 above most are self explanatory as they list the basic facts and details of the person making the claim and on whose behalf the claim is made.

Points 11, 12 and 17 are the most troublesome.

Suggested commentary could be:-

For point 11 :- (Mrs X requires 24 E.M.I. care)
(Mrs X suffers from Vascular Dementia /Alzheimer's Disease as the case may be)
(Mrs X suffers from a condition which is terminal)
(The mental health of Mrs X is so poor that it was necessary to apply for the

registration of her Enduring Power of Attorney with the Court)

(The mental health of Mrs X is such that it was necessary to apply for the appointment of a Receiver to take control and manage her affairs.

(Mrs X suffered a sever stroke which rendered her totally incapacitated and immobile).

(Mrs X is doubly incontinent)

(Mrs X Fulfils Eligibility Criteria for full NHS Funding as per Coughlan case of 1999 and also Ombudsman Rulings regarding patients suffering from Vascular Dementia /Severe Stoke as the case may be).

As many points as possible should be included in the list but be as accurate as possible.

For point 12 :- This section is to include other important points that are not entered elsewhere. On most occasions there will be nothing further to add.

One example may be to say that the care funding assessment plays down or misrepresents the actual level of health suffered.

Another relevant comment would be if the person has not been placed in the type of care home recommended by a doctor or consultant.

For point 17 :- Admittance to care without correct assessment / application of eligibility criteria as set out in 1999 Coughlan court ruling on long term care for those whose needs are primarily health care orientated and also decisions of Health Service Ombudsman indicate that Mrs X should have been assessed as qualifying for full NHS funding from the time of admittance to care as a result of Vascular Dementia/Severe Stroke/Alzheimer's Disease.

And/or

The level of NHS banding contribution being paid is not at the correct level taking into account the high level of care being provided by care and nursing staff.

LIST OF STATUTES

The following statutes are a list of the main laws which are relevant when a discussion of liability for care costs arises. Please remember however that the applicable law also includes case law. These are cases which have been brought before the courts and judges have had to decide on points of law. These cases are also known as the common law.

Statutes and cases may change how matters are dealt with by Councils and the other relevant authorities;

The main statutes are:-

The National Health Service and Community Care Act 1990

The National Assistance Act 1948

The Health Services and Public Health Act 1968 Section 45

The Chronically Sick and Disabled Persons Act 1970 Section 2

The National Health Service Act 1977 Section 21 and Schedule 8

Mental Health Act 1983 Section 117

The Health and Social Services and Social Security Adjudications Act 1983 Part 7

The Disabled Persons (Services Consultation and Representation) Act 1986

The Insolvency Act 1986

The Carers (Recognition and Services) Act 1995

The Community Care (Direct Payments) Act 1996

The Housing Grants, Construction and Regeneration Act 1996

The National Health Service (Primary Care) Act 1997

The (Community Care Residential Accommodation) Act 1998

The Housing Act 1996 Part 7

The Human Rights Act 1998

The Health Act 1999

The Carers and Disabled Children Act 2000

The Care Standards Act 2000

The Health and Social Care Act 2001 Part 4

The National Health Service Reform and Healthcare Professions Act 2002 Part 1

Community Care (Delayed Discharges) Act 2003

The Health and Social Care (Community Health Standards) Act 2003

Carers (Equal Opportunities) Act 2004

Mental Capacity Act 2005

By implication other legislation is also involved in any assessment for the provision of community care services.

For example:-

Local Government Act 1970

Local Authority Social Services Act 1970 (LASSA)

Pensions Act 1995

Disability Discrimination Act 1995

The Data Protection Act 1998

The Welfare Reform and Pensions Act 1999

The Freedom of Information Act 2000

INDEX TO PRECEDENTS

1). Notice of Severance of Joint Tenancy.

2). Will clause as confirmation/evidence of Declaration of Trust.

3). Will clause as confirmation/evidence of Proprietary Estopple.

4). Deed of Disclaimer.

5). Deed of Variation.

6). Will clause of a life interest.

7). Declaration of Trust.

8). Enduring Power of Attorney.

PRECEDENTS

These precedents are intended as examples of what each relevant document looks like and includes. Individual circumstances will vary from person to person and so amendments will need to be made to accurately reflect the true situation in each case. Legal advice should be obtained as to the content of any legal document that is prepared.

The precedents themselves are best set out as A4 size documents.

1). **SEVERANCE OF JOINT TENANCY**

If typed on a sheet of A4 paper the full text should cover one page.

NOTICE OF SEVERANCE OF JOINT TENANCY

1. (a) We *[full name of first joint owner]* and *[full name of second joint owner]* are the joint owners of the property described in the Schedule hereto ("the Property")

   (b) We hold the property and the future proceeds of sale on behalf of ourselves as beneficial joint tenants so that in the event of the death of either of us the survivor will become the sole owner

2. We understand that having regard to the considerations of Inheritance Tax and our future financial planning, it would be preferable to convert our beneficial joint tenancy into a tenancy in common so that we each have the right in future to dispose of our individual interests in the Property and its proceeds of sale under our respective Wills

3. Accordingly by virtue of the proviso to Section 36(2) of the Law of Property Act 1925, each of us hereby gives notice to the other of our desire to sever as from the date of this notice our joint tenancy in equity over the Property and we separately declare that the joint tenancy is thereby duly severed in equity to the intent that we shall from the date of this notice hold the Property and the future proceeds of sale as tenants in common in equal shares

The Schedule (above referred to)

ALL THAT piece or parcel of Freehold/Leasehold land together with dwellinghouse erected thereon and known as *[Full postal address of property]*.

Dated this……………..……day of………..……………2006

………………………………… …………………………….
1st Joint Tenant   **2nd Joint Tenant**

END

2). **WILL CLAUSE in confirmation of existence of Declaration of Trust**

This clause should appear before any other dispositions in the will. This will probably be following any expression of funeral arrangements and if there are none after the latter of the clause appointing the Executors and or Guardians.

Situation 1 - Freehold Property

<u>**I GIVE AND DEVISE**</u> all my share and interest in my Freehold dwellinghouse situate at and known as *[insert address of property]* to such of them *[insert names and addresses of those named as beneficiaries in Declaration of Trust Deed]* as tenants in common in equal shares absolutely in accordance with the terms of the Declaration of Trust Deed dated *[insert date of Deed]*

Situation 2 - Leasehold Property

<u>**I GIVE AND BEQUEATH**</u> all my share and interest in my Leasehold dwellinghouse situate at and known as *[insert address of property]* to such of them *[insert names and addresses of those named as beneficiaries in Declaration of Trust Deed]* as tenants in common in equal shares absolutely in accordance with the terms of the Declaration of Deed Trust *[insert date of Deed]*

Notes:-

1). *If there is only one beneficiary then the clause should be amended by deleting the words to such of them .... as tenants in common in equal shares.*

2).   *The relationships (if any) of the beneficiary(s) should be included. For example I GIVE ….. to such of them my son……and my daughter……….*

3).   *Do not add any further provisions to the clause to deal with the situation that a beneficiary may die first. This is not necessary because the interest held by the beneficiary will form part of his or her estate. Consequently such provision should be dealt with the beneficiaries will. Furthermore if you are saying that the property belongs to the beneficiary then it is not yours to pass to anyone else. To make comment on this undermines the trust arrangement.*

END

3). **WILL CLAUSE in confirmation of Proprietary Estoppel**

The clause will be the same as for the Declaration of Trust above apart from the replacement of the words "in accordance with the terms of the Declaration of Trust Deed dated.." with "in satisfaction of their Propriety Estoppel (being an equitable interest) in the said *[insert address of property]*

Notes.

1). *The expenditure on the property required to create the proprietary estoppel does not have to take place before the will is signed. This is because the will speaks from death and so relates to the position at the time of death. Therefore by the time of death and thus the time the will comes into effect the proprietary estoppel will have been created.*

2). *Similarly as in the case of the Declaration of Trust there should be no reference to who would then benefit if the holder of the proprietary estoppel died first for the same reasons.*

END

4). DISCLAIMER

Situation 1 - The gift is contained in a will

BY THIS DEED I the undersigned *[insert full name of person disclaiming]* **of** *[insert address of person disclaiming]* **hereby disclaim all benefit under the devise/bequest in my favour contained in the will of** *[insert name of deceased]* **dated** *[insert date of will]* **and proved in the** *[insert the name of the probate registry which issued the probate]* **of the Family Division of the High Court of Justice on the** *[insert date probate issued]* **to** *[insert names of Executors]* **the Executors therein mentioned and I also disclaim all estate and interest in the Residuary Estate of the said** *[insert name of deceased]*.

IN WITNESS WHEREOF I have executed these presents as my deed this   day of   20..

SIGNED and delivered as a deed by the)
said *[insert name of person disclaiming)* **)**
in the presence of:-

END

Situation 2 - There is no will and so the beneficiary of the gift is entitled under the Intestacy Rules

BY THIS DEED I the undersigned *[insert full name of person disclaiming]* of *[insert address of person disclaiming]* hereby disclaim all benefit and entitlement which is due to me as *[insert relationship to deceased eg wife, son, daughter as the case may be]* of *[insert name of deceased]* which is due to me by virtue of the provisions of The Administration of Estates Act 1925 and especially Section 46 thereof a grant of Letters of Administration to the estate was granted on *[insert date of issue of the grant]* by the *[insert the name of the probate registry which issued the probate]* of the Family Division of the High Court of Justice to *[insert names of Administrators]*.

IN WITNESS WHEREOF I have executed these presents as my deed this   day of   20..

SIGNED and delivered as a deed by the)
said *[insert name of person disclaiming*)
in the presence of:-

END

Notes.

1. *Although there is no legal requirement for a Disclaimer to be in writing it is better to be evidenced in writing to avoid future difficulty.*

2. *Where a gift comprises several parts it is not possible for only a part of the gift to be disclaimed. It is a question of all or nothing.*

3. *If a Disclaimer is unsuitable for any reason consider the alternative of a deed of variation.*

END

5). DEED OF VARIATION

The following precedent is only an example. For fuller details of Deeds of Variation please refer to the Post Death Variations section of a suitable practitioner's text book such as Williams on Wills. The ISBN number for this two volume set is 0-406-93391-X. It can usually be found in a large law library.

The situation dealt with by the Variation below is where one spouse has died and the freehold house passes to the surviving spouse by right of survivorship. The Deed therefore deals with the splitting of the property into two so that one half forms part of the estate of the deceased spouse and the second is what is to be done with the deceased spouse's half of the property. The gift is a life interest trust to allow the surviving spouse the use of the trust half. If the deceased spouse has debts or the value of the estate of the surviving spouse including the full value of the property exceeds the Inheritance Tax threshold figure (£285,000 for 2006/07) then this type of variation will not be suitable. Instead a Variation that includes a Discretionary Trust with full trust and administrative provisions is required.

THIS DEED OF VARIATION is made this

day of   Two thousand and Six Between *[insert name of widow]* of *[insert address of widow]* (hereinafter called "the widow") of the one part and *[insert name of intended long term beneficiary]* of *[insert address) of beneficiary]* *[add the names and addresses of any other beneficiaries]* (hereinafter called "the beneficiary(s)") of the other part

WHEREAS

(A) Immediately prior to the death on the *[insert date of late husbands death]* of *[insert full name of late husband* (hereinafter called "the deceased") the deceased and the widow held the property (hereinafter called "the Property") known as *[insert address of property]* upon trust to sell the same and to hold the net proceeds of sale thereof for themselves as beneficial joint tenants.

(B) Following the death of the deceased the widow is absolutely entitled to the Property by right of survivorship.

(C) The widow desires to vary the disposition of the deceased's severable share in the Property (or the net proceeds of sale thereof) effected by right of survivorship so as to benefit the beneficiaries in the manner hereinafter appearing.

(D) The last will and testament of the deceased dated the *[insert date of will]* has not as yet been proved

OR

(D) The last will and testament of the deceased was proved on the *[insert date of issue of probate]* in the *[insert name of probate registry which issued the probate]* by *[insert names of Executors]*

(E) The said will of the deceased bequeaths unto the

widow all the residue of his real and personal estate absolutely

NOW THIS DEED WITNESSES AS FOLLOWS:-

1. The widow and beneficiary hereby agree and declare by way of variation of the disposition of the deceased's severable share in the Property (or the net proceeds of sale thereof) which took effect on the deceased's death by right of survivorship as follows:-

(1) That it shall be deemed that the beneficial joint tenancy of the deceased and the widow in the Property (or the net proceeds of sale thereof) had been severed immediately prior to the death of the deceased so that immediately prior to the death of the deceased he and the widow held the Property upon trust to sell the same and to hold the net proceeds of sale thereof for themselves as beneficial tenants in common in equal shares.

(2) That the deceased's deemed one-half share in the Property (or the net proceeds of sale thereof) as aforesaid shall be deemed to have been disposed of by a will made by the deceased as the same now appears below (subject to the payment of any inheritance tax attributable thereto on or by reason

of his death) and the widow shall henceforth hold the Property upon trust to sell the same and to hold the net proceeds of sale thereof for himself and the estate of the deceased as beneficial tenants in common in equal shares.

(3) That in substitution for the absolute gift in favour of the widow the Will of the deceased as bequeathed by clause *[insert the number of the clause which includes the gift to the widow]* therein that the will shall contain the following powers and provisions:-

    1(A). **I GIVE AND DEVISE** all my share and interest in my Freehold dwellinghouse situate at and known as *[insert address of property]* (hereinafter called "the Property") to my Trustees upon trust with the written consent of my wife *[insert full name of widow]* during her life to sell the same with full power to postpone such sale and to pay the income of the proceeds of the sale of the Property to the said *[insert name of widow]* during her life

    (B). **MY TRUSTEES** may invest the proceeds of sale of the Property and any other capital moneys subject to the foregoing trusts of this Clause in any assets of any description or location whatever and may change any such assets for any other such assets to the intent that they shall have the powers of investment and changing investments of a sole beneficial owner

(C). **WITHOUT PREJUDICE** to the generality of the last foregoing subclause of this Clause my Trustees may apply the proceeds of sale of the Property or any other capital moneys subject to the foregoing trusts of this Clause in the purchase or improvement of any house anywhere in the world (including the purchase of any estate or interest in any house) for residence therein by the said *[insert name of widow]* under the power set out below and any house or estate or interest in any house purchased under the foregoing power shall be held on the same trusts and with and subject to the same powers and provisions (including the requirement of the written consent of the said *[insert name of widow]* to a sale) as those provided herein in relation to the Property (or as near thereto as the local law shall permit)

(D). **MY TRUSTEES** may permit or join in permitting the said *[insert name of widow]* to reside in any house which or any estate or interest in which is for the time being subject to the foregoing trusts of this Clause upon such conditions as to insurance repair payment of rent rates or other outgoings and generally upon such terms (if any) as my Trustees think fit and my Trustees shall not be liable for any failure to pay outgoings or insure or repair if the said *[insert name of widow]* is responsible for the same under the terms of such residence

(E). **SUBJECT** as aforesaid my Trustees shall hold the proceeds of sale of the Property and the income thereon **UPON TRUST** for such of them my *[insert names of beneficiaries as detailed above]* as shall survive me and the said *[insert names of widow]* and if more than one as tenants in common in equal shares absolutely **PROVIDED THAT** if any such son or daughter of mine shall have died in my lifetime or having survived me shall fail to survive the said *[insert name of widow]* in either case leaving a child or children living at the death of the survivor of myself and the said *[insert name of widow]* who attain the age of twenty one years then such child or children shall take by substitution and if more than one as tenants in common in equal shares absolutely the share of the property which his her or their deceased parent would have taken had he or she survived me and the said *[insert name of widow]*

(F).   IN this clause:

    (a) 'house' includes flat

    (b) references to the proceeds of sale of the Property include the assets from time to time representing the same;

    (c) references to the income of the proceeds of sale of the Property include the net rents and profits until sale thereof;

    (d) references to any house include any ancillary land or buildings enjoyed therewith;

    (e) references to an interest in a house include an interest in the proceeds of sale thereof;

(f) where an estate or interest in a house is held on the trusts of this Clause the same consent shall be required for my Trustees to concur with other owners of estates or interests therein in a sale of such house as is required for sale of the estate therein which is subject to the trusts of this Clause

3. **SUBJECT** as aforesaid and to the payment of my funeral and testamentary expenses and debts **I GIVE** all my property and assets of every kind and wherever situated to my wife the said *[insert name of widow]* absolutely

4. **IN ADDITION** to all other powers conferred by law or under this my will my Trustees (not being less than two in number) shall have power during the lifetime of my wife the said *[insert name of widow]* to raise capital out of the proceeds of sale of the Property for the following purposes:-

(i) For the purpose of paying or applying the same to or for the benefit of the said *[insert name of widow]*

(ii) For the purpose of making loans to the said

[insert name of widow] either with or without security and with or without interest and generally upon such terms and subject to such conditions as my Trustees shall in their absolute discretion think fit and **I HEREBY EXPRESSLY DECLARE** that my Trustees shall have complete freedom to make loans to the said *[insert name of widow]* and to leave any such loans outstanding during her lifetime and my Trustees shall not be liable for any loss that may be occasioned to the proceeds of sale of the Property from any cause whatsoever in respect of the making of any such loans and the failure to recover the amounts thereby due to be repaid whether before or after the death of the said *[insert name of widow]*

AND I DECLARE that when considering whether or not to exercise the foregoing powers for the benefit of the said *[insert name of widow]* my Trustees shall disregard the interests of any other beneficiaries in the proceeds of sale of the property

(4). The parties hereto certify that this instrument falls within category M in the Schedule to the Stamp

Duty (Exempt Instruments) Regulations 1987.

(5). The parties hereto give notice to the Board of Inland Revenue in accordance with section 142(2) of the Inheritance Tax Act 1984 and section 62(7) of the Taxation of Chargeable Gains Act 1992 that they elect that the provisions of Section 142(1) thereof and section 62(6) thereof respectively shall apply to this variation as such provisions made by this deed within two years of the death of the deceased.

(OR IF THE DEED IS SIGNED AFTER THE SECOND ANNIVERSARY OF THE HUSBANDS DEATH)

(5). The parties hereto do not give notice to the Board of Inland Revenue in accordance with section 142(2) of the Inheritance Tax Act 1984 and section 62(7) of the Taxation of Chargeable Gains Act 1992 that they elect that the provisions of Section 142(1) thereof and section 62(6) thereof respectively as such provisions made by this deed were entered into after two years from the date of death of the deceased.

IN WITNESS whereof the parties hereto have signed their names on the day and date hereinbefore written

Signed as a deed and delivered)
by *(insert name of widow)*)
in the presence of)

                                    Witness

Signature

Name

Address

Occupation

Signed as a deed and delivered)
by *(insert name of beneficiary)*)
in the presence of)

                                    Witness

Signature

Name

Address

Occupation

END

Notes.

1. *Many other matters may be included in the Variation such as an additional Trust to protect money and or other investments held by the deceased in addition to the house. This may also include money held in a joint bank account or joint shareholding.*

2. *The problems arising as a result of any errors when preparing a Variation would justify the costs involved in seeking professional advice even if were to check the content of the Variation .*

END

6). **WILL CLAUSE giving a life interest.**

The clause detailed in the Variation above shows the relevant clause however the following additional clause should be included as subclause (ii) if this clause is incorporated into a will:-

(ii) **IF** by the time of my death I shall have sold my interest in the said house or shall have an estate or interest therein different from that which I have at the date of this Will then this Clause shall have effect as if there were substituted for the reference in the last foregoing subclause to my interest in the said house a reference to all the estate or interest (if any) which I shall have at my death in the house which at my death is my only or main residence

END

Notes.

1. *This additional subclause is to deal with the possibility that the couple may move address after the will is signed. Therefore a new will would not need to be made. The new property would however need to be bought as tenants in common..*

END

7). **DECLARATION OF TRUST**

The example given below is for the most common type of situation namely the purchase of a council house or indeed any other property where the purchase money and or any mortgage installments and or any other capital expenditure on the property after completion is being provided by one or more other persons (usually children as an investment) and the buyer wishes to protect the interest of those providing that funding or other financial assistance.

THIS DECLARATION OF TRUST is made this day of   Two thousand and six by *[insert name of council house tenant(s) buying the property]* of *[insert address of buyer(s)]* (hereinafter called "the Trustee(s)") of the first part and *[insert names and addressed of all persons providing purchase funds]* (hereinafter called "the Beneficiary(ies)") of the other part

WHEREAS

1.   BY a Transfer dated *[insert date of completion of the purchase]* the property more particularly described in the First Schedule hereto was vested in the Trustee(s) in fee simple

2.   TO assist in the purchase, the Trustee(s) received a capital sum of *[insert amount of capital sum provided by beneficiary(ies)]* from the beneficiaries in full payment of

the purchase price for the property as paid to *[insert name of Council to whom purchase price paid]* under the council house right to buy legislation.

OR

2. TO assist in the purchase the beneficiary(ies) have agreed to provide funds to enable payment in full of the monthly mortgage installments which become due and are payable to *[insert name of mortgage lender]* in accordance with the terms of the mortgage.

3. TO assist in the purchase the Beneficiary(ies) also provided all other costs of purchase as set out on the completion statement.

4. THE beneficiary(ies) are the *[insert relationship of beneficiary(ies) to Trustee(s)]* of the Trustee(s) *[insert the following if there are others in the same class who have not joined in with the purchase]* :- and the other children of the Trustee(s) namely …………. were aware of the purchase and raised no objection to the purchase and they also declined to be a party to the purchase.

5. THE beneficiaries have agreed to discharge all property insurance, maintenance, repair and improvements costs that may arise from time to time.

6. IN consideration of the payment of the said Capital sum/mortgage installments plus other related costs to date and future expenditure and the agreement and actions of the beneficiary(ies) the Trustee(s) have agreed to Execute this Deed to record the true beneficial interest which is applicable to the Property by virtue of the constructive trust that exists in favour of the beneficiary(ies) and also as a result of the proprietary estoppel held as an equitable interest by the Beneficiary(ies) in the Property.

NOW THIS DEED WITNESSETH as follows:-

1. THE TRUSTEE(s) hereby declare(s) that the net proceeds of sale after repayment of any mortgage, maintenance charges, estate agent fees, legal costs and any other sums due on sale or otherwise charged as security over the Property are held by the Trustee(s) for the benefit of the Beneficiary(ies) or their respective heirs.

2. IT IS HEREBY DECLARED that the Trustee(s) shall have full power during the period of his/her/their occupation of the property and or as holder of the legal estate in the property to mortgage charge lease or otherwise dispose of all or any part of the Property for full

consideration with all powers in that behalf of an absolute owner.

3. THE BENEFICIARY(IES) understand(s) and agree(s) that he/she/they will take no action during the lifetime of the Trustee(s) to enforce the power of sale created by this trust deed.

4. THE TRUSTEE(S) understand(s) agree(s) and approve(s) of a future transfer of the Legal title to the Beneficiary(ies) by any person or persons (including the Beneficiary(ies) himself/herself/themselves) acting under the authority of an Enduring Power of Attorney should the situation arise that the Trustee(s) is/are no longer capable of residing in the Property and or of managing his/her/their legal and financial affairs.

5. FOR THE avoidance of doubt the parties hereby declare that this deed is intended to create legal relations between them and as such is binding and enforceable in law and in equity.

6. THE TRUSTEE(S) acknowledge(s) to have received independent legal advice as to his/her/their position and is/are desirous of recognizing and protecting the equitable interest in the property held by the Beneficiary(ies).

IN WITNESS whereof the parties have hereunto signed this Deed the day and year hereinbefore mentioned.

THE FIRST SCHEDULE hereinbefore referred to
ALL THAT piece or parcel of Freehold land/Leasehold flat together with dwellinghouse erected thereon situate at and known as *[insert full postal address of property]* which Property is more particularly described and delineated on the plan annexed to the Title Information Document/Charge Certificate/Land Certificate and the title to which is registered at H M Land Registry.

SIGNED AS A DEED by the said)
[insert name of Trustee]   )
in the presence of:-

[add same for all other parties to the deed]

END

8). ENDURING POWER OF ATTORNEY

This is a set form by law as contained in the Enduring Powers of Attorney Act 1985. The form which is in A4 size format can be downloaded from the Public Guardianship Office Web-site or obtained as a pre-printed form from a legal stationery supplier.

Of note however is that the personal details on the form contain a space on the third page as follows:-

"Subject to the following restrictions and conditions:"

If this is deleted then the Power comes into effect immediately it is signed. This may be appropriate if the person granting the Power (called the Donor) is elderly and housebound as it will enable day to day financial matters to be attended too without great delay or difficulty.

However if the Power is being granted by parents to one or more of their children (even including the other spouse) and the children and especially if the children are still relatively young then the granting of such a blanket authority is likely to be less appropriate. Therefore consider including a restriction in the Power such as the following:-

"That my Attorney(s) shall not act on my behalf unless and until they have reason to believe that I am becoming mentally incapable and or that I am suffering from some form of physical incapacity which prevents me from communicating my wishes in regard to the management of my legal and financial affairs."

In practice the Attorney(s) may be required to obtain a letter from the donor's G.P. or other medical practitioner confirming the nature of the incapacity giving rise to why the Attorney(s) seek to make use of the Power.

The law on Powers of Attorney is to change significantly in that from April 2007 Enduring Powers of Attorney will be replaced by Lasting Powers of Attorney. Existing Enduring Powers will continue to be effective.

END

INDEX

24 HOUR CARE	19, 24, 121
ABUSE	43
ABUSE OF POWER	41, 92
ACTION ON ELDER ABUSE	43
ADMINISTRATION OF ESTATES ACT	127
ADMINISTRATOR	28
AFFORDABILITY	44
ALTERNATIVE DISPUTE RESOLUTION	52, 82
ALZHEIMER'S DISEASE	27
ANNUITY	45
APPEAL PROCESS	34
APPLICABLE LAWS	162
APPOINTEE	28
ATTENDANCE ALLOWANCE	37, 47
ATTITUDE	57
ATTORNEY	35
AVOIDANCE	148
BANDING SYSTEM	20
BANK ACCOUNT	71
BANKRUPTCY	57, 75
BENEFICIAL OWNERSHIP	51
BUSINESS INTERESTS	46
CAPITAL GAINS TAX	75
CAPITAL GAINS TAX PLANNING	147
CARE BY CHILDREN	111
CARE CHARGES	15
CARE FEE INSURANCE	47
CARE REFUND CLAIM FORM	162
CARER	48, 49
CASH WITHDRAWALS	72
CAUTION	116
CENTRAL LONDON PROPERTY TRUST v HIGH TREES HOUSE 1947	100
CITIZENS ADVICE BUREAU	35
CIVIL PARTNERSHIP ACT 2004	85, 138
CIVIL WRONG	78
COMPLAINTS	148
COMPLEX NEEDS	22
CONFIDENTIALITY	149
CONFISCATION OF ASSETS	66

CONFLICT OF INTEREST	48
CONSENT FORM	33
CONSIDERATION	78, 110
CONSTRUCTIVE TRUST	49
CONSUMER ORGANISATION	31, 35
CONTINUING CARE BED	18
CONTRACT	78
COUGHLAN CASE	25, 150
COUNCIL HOUSE PURCHASE	50, 76
COUNCILS	149
COURT	52
COURT ACTION	79
CRAG	150
CRIMINAL LAW	66
DATA PROTECTION REGISTRAR	149
DEATH	57
DECLARATION OF TRUST	51, 52, 109
DEED OF DISCLAIMER	95
DEED OF VARIATION	55, 95, 127
DEFENDANT	79
DEGRADING TREATMENT	64
DEMENTIA	27
DISCLAIMER	53, 95
DISCRETIONARY TRUST	56, 97, 104
DISCRIMINATION	69, 118
DISTRICT LAND REGISTRY	77
DIVORCE	56, 75
DUEL REGISTERED HOME	18
ELIGIBILITY CRITERIA	23, 26, 69
EMI HOME	18
ENDURING POWER OF ATTORNEY	28, 40, 51, 80, 114, 151
ENGLISH LAW	69
EQUITABLE INTERESTS	107
EQUITY RELEASE	57
EUROPEAN LAW	69
EUROPEAN UNION	45
EXECUTOR	28, 40
EXPRESSION OF WISH FORM	97
FAIRNESS	81
FAMILY BUSINESS	46
FAMILY LAW REFORM ACT 1969	54
FAMILY LIFE	67

FOUL PLAY	152
FREEDOM OF INFORMATION ACT 2000	152
FREEHOLD PROPERTY	59
FUNERAL PLANS	60
GIVING AWAY ASSETS	74
HEALTH CARE COMPONENT	37
HEALTH SERVICE OMBUDSMAN	33
HEALTHCARE COMMISSION	61
HIGH BAND CARE	22
HIGH TREES HOUSE CASE	100
HOLIDAYS	122
HOME CARE	62, 99
HOSPICE	18
HUMAN RIGHTS ACT - Article 1	63
HUMAN RIGHTS ACT - Article 3	64
HUMAN RIGHTS ACT - Article 5	65
HUMAN RIGHTS ACT - Article 7	66
HUMAN RIGHTS ACT - Article 8	67
HUMAN RIGHTS ACT - Article 14	69
ICEBURG	107
IGNORANCE OF THE LAW	94
IMPROVEMENT IN HEALTH	23
INCOME SUPPORT	153
INDEPENDENT FINANCIAL ADVISER	70, 74
INDEPENDENT LEGAL ADVICE	92
INDIRECT TAXES	17
INDIVIDUALS HOME	15
INHERITANCE TAX	55, 96, 97
INHERITANCE TAX PLANNING	57, 143, 158
INSURANCE POLICY	47
INTEREST	30
INTESTACY RULES	55, 127
INTRODUCTION	11
INVESTMENT	69
JOINT BANK ACCOUNT	71
LAND LAW	107
LAND REGISTRY	112
LAW CENTRE	35
LAW OF PROPERTY ACT 1925	52
LAWYER	40
LEASEHOLD PROPERTY	59
LEGAL ADVICE	155
LEGAL INTERESTS	107

LEGAL OWNER	51
LEGAL REPRSENTATIVE	28
LEGITIMATE EXPECTATION	41
LIBERTY AND SECURITY	65
LICENSE	72
LIFE EXPECTANCY	15, 39
LIFE INSUARCE	73
LIFE INTEREST TRUST	104
LIFE POLICY	73
LIFETIME GIFTS	74, 76
LIFETIME MORTGAGE	59
LIMITATION ACT 1980	78
LITIGATION	79
LOCAL COUNCILLOR	83
LORD SCARMAN	81
LOW BAND CARE	21
MALCOLM POINTON	63, 99
MARKET VALUE	87
MARRIAGE	83
MATRIMONIAL HOME	56
MEDICAL ADVICE	89
MEDICAL NEGLIGENCE	86
MEDIUM BAND CARE	22
MENTAL CAPACITY ACT 2005	155
MENTAL HEALTH ACT 1983	86
MISCELLANEOUS MATTERS	148
MORE TROUBLE THAN ITS WORTH	155
MORTGAGE INSTALMENTS	49
MOVE HOUSE	86
MP	31, 82
MUTUAL WILL	131
NATIONAL ASSISTANCE ACT 1948	85, 90, 137
NATIONAL HEALTH SERVICE AND COMMUNITY CARE ACT 1990	90
NATIONAL HEALTH SERVICE	103
NATIONAL INSURANCE CONTRIBUTIONS	17, 41, 102
NEGLIGENCE	31, 92
NEXT OF KIN	29
NHS BANDING PAYMENT	22
NHS CONTINUING CARE BED	18
NHS ELIGIBILITY ASSESSMENT	41
NHS ESTABLISHMENTS	18, 19
NHS FUNDING CLAIM	88

NHS FUNDING	23
NOMINATION	97
NURSING CARE HOME	18
NURSING CARE	21
OBTAINING MONEY BY DECEPTION	124
OPTIONS	41
PALFREY CASE	96
PEACEFUL ENJOYMENT	63
PENSION CREDIT	153
PENSION FUND	97
PERSONAL INJURY	99
PERSONAL INJURY TRUST	99
PERSONAL REPRESENTATIVE	28
PLAINTIFF	79
POCKET MONEY	38, 135
POINTON CASE	63, 99
POST CODE LOTTERY	26
PRE-PAID FUNERAL	60, 122
PRIMARY CARE TRUST	26, 28
PRIVATE LIFE	67
PROBATE PROCEDURES	157
PROFESSIONAL COSTS	35
PROFESSIONAL EXECUTOR	160
PROMISSORY ESTOPPEL	100
PROPERTY REPAIR	49
PROPRIETARY ESTOPPEL	106, 143, 147
PROTECTION OF CAPITAL ASSETS	39
PROTECTION OF FUTURE ASSETS	141
PROTECTION OF INCOME	134
PUBLIC GUARDIANSHIP OFFICE	81, 113
PUBLIC INTEREST	115
PUBLIC POLICY	115
PUBLICITY	157
PURCHASE MONEY	49
RE-ASSESSMENT	158
RECEIVER	28, 40, 80, 113
REDUNDANCY	57, 75
REFUND	29
REFUND CLAIM	33
REFUND CLAIM TIMING	158
REFUSAL TO PAY	116
RESPECT FOR FAMILY LIFE	67
RESPECT FOR PRIVATE LIFE	67

RESIDENTIAL CARE HOME	17
RESIDENTIAL CARE	19
RESULTING TRUST	49
RESPITE	15
REVIEW PANEL	34
RIGHT OF RESIDENCE	104
ROYAL COMMISSION	82, 115
SCOTTISH SYSTEM	118
SELF FUNDING	37
SEVERANCE OF JOINT TENANCY	118
SHELTERED ACCOMODATION	158
SHORTHOLD TENANCY AGREEMENT	73
SOCIAL CARE	120
SOCIAL SECURITY	154
SOCIAL SERVICES	24
SOLE NAME PROPERTY	103
SPEND MONEY	121
STATE BENEFITS	19
STATUTE BARRED	78
STATUTES	162
STRATEGIC AREA HEALTH AUTHORITY	33
STRENGTH IN NUMBERS	159
STROKE	27
SURVIVING SPOUSE	95
TAX PLANNING	106
TAXABLE INCOME	45
TAXES	41
THEFT	123
THEFT ACT 1968	123
TIMESCALE	30
TORT	78
TOWNSON V TICKELL 1819	53, 128
TRADE UNION	35
TRUSTS OF LAND AND APPOINTMENT OF TRUSTEES ACT 1996	126
TRUSTS	125
UNFAIRNESS	17
UNIVERSITY FEES	66
UNMARRIED PARTNERS	85
UNPAID CARE	111
UNREGISTRED LAND	77
UPPER THRESHOLD	60
VARIATION	55, 95, 127